The Student Revolt

The Seventh Bowl

The Student Revolt

COLIN CROUCH

THE BODLEY HEAD
LONDON SYDNEY
TORONTO

For Joan

© Colin Crouch 1970
ISBN 0 370 01320 4
Printed and bound in Great Britain for
The Bodley Head Ltd
9 Bow Street, London WC2
by William Clowes & Sons Ltd, Beccles
Set in Monotype Baskerville 169
First published 1970

CONTENTS

5

In a way, of course, all this has to do with the great Weberian themes and we must recognise the valid elements in the current protest. It attempts to counteract acquiescence, consensus politics, the divisive character of multiplying roles, anonymity, the elongated structure of bureaucratic power, indeed the whole process of rationalisation conceived of apart from overriding human purposes. It rejects knowledge without understanding, process without community, power without purpose.

Weber argued that an indirect mutation of the Protestant spirit was essential to the birth of the modern world of capitalism and bureaucracy. By a curious irony it is an indirect mutation of capitalism and bureaucracy which produces the protesting spirit, not now canalised and distorted either by the psychic disciplines of capitalist accumulation or by the work disciplines of industrialism, but in a world of increasing automation and leisure able again to ask its own proper question: "What is the chief end of Man?"

(David Martin, "The Dissolution of the Monasteries", from *Anarchy and Culture*, 1969)

6

Introduction

The bare skeleton of the argument to be presented in this book is as follows: as a result of certain developments taking place in the political structures of western societies, particularly those developments relating to the increasing importance of technological growth and economic planning, far-left opposition to the political establishment has adopted a novel form. In the case of Britain this whole process is intimately bound up with the accession to power of a Labour Government in 1964. One area where these developments have made themselves felt is the university. Since university institutions are places where the new perspectives of the far left can be put into practice more easily than elsewhere, the universities have tended to bear the brunt of this wider political dissent.

Within the university this dissent appears to centre on three related issues: a crisis of authority, a search for "community", and concern for the relationship between the university and the forces of state and industry. These three areas have certain implications for the wider political stance of the new left, and in particular lead to certain peculiarities in its own organisation and sources of cohesion.

My main concern is to achieve some understanding of this movement, of the motivations that impel it, the sources of its dissent, the forms of its activities, and its major objectives. In so doing, however, we shall also have cause to examine for their own sake some of the issues on which the left has concentrated its attention, both within the universities and in the outside political world.

First, I consider very briefly the major political events and facts that appear to be most salient to radical youth in Britain. This assists a preliminary understanding of the kind of issue to which they are likely to respond, and the direction of their response. I then examine, in much more detail, the history of student revolt at the London School of Economics and Political Science.

The strong emphasis on this one college is partly justified by the fact that it has set the lead among British universities in the growth of a movement of student revolt and was the first institution in Britain to feel the currents of a movement that had already achieved importance in the USA, West Germany and Japan. However, the main reason for the prominence of the LSE is that I have been able to study revolt there from the outset, initially as protagonist and finally as antagonist.

The main task of these two chapters, and the succeeding one which attempts to summarise more cursorily events at other British universities, is to provide a reflective narrative. The concern is not simply to relate the events that occurred, but to try to understand them in the context in which they occurred, and to study the processes of organisation and development that have taken place.

In this way these narrative chapters pave the way for the discussions in Part II, where I attempt to analyse student revolt in terms of two major theoretical concepts – authority and "community" – and then to relate the university to the outside world in those areas where it is of most relevance to the student protest movement. In this way it is possible to provide an analysis of the structure and perspectives of student revolt movements and to relate them more directly than was possible at the outset to certain political themes. This is then taken up in more detail in Chapter Eight, where we move from consideration of the university to a study of some of the wider political problems in the past few years on which the movement of student dissent has nourished itself.

These are issues of greater magnitude and importance than student revolt itself, and our consideration of them must obviously be cursory and nothing like so detailed. If this section achieves anything it will not be as a definitive discussion of the problems of modern politics, but simply as a more explicit discussion of the background to student revolt, and, more ambitiously, to pose in a useful way some of the questions that now need to be answered.

The book hovers a little uneasily between subjective and obviously biased reminiscence and a sociological analysis which pretends to a certain degree of rigour and objectivity. This combination was inevitable, given my own position. As someone who has taken some part in the whole affair at the LSE, it would have been unreal to have presented simply an impersonal discussion of the matter, adopting the relation to the subject of the neutral scientific observer. On the other hand, it would have been wrong simply to present a narrative when I find sociological concepts extremely valuable in analysing and understanding the various phenomena. Revolutionaries will possibly applaud my readiness to learn from "praxis" and the "real" world of experience and action, though they will look darkly on my willingness to allow my free sense experience to be distorted by the conspiracies and mystifications of bourgeois sociology.

Critics of a different sort will similarly frown on the use of such words as "legitimacy", "charisma", "Gemeinschaft". I can only hope that for once they will be prepared to suspend their mistrust of sociology's attempt to use its own analytical tools and will judge whether the use of such concepts assists in bringing order to refractory material. Further critics will excuse sociological jargon, but will disapprove of attempts to draw theoretical conclusions from evidence gathered in such a non-rigorous way. This is a criticism I readily accept, but in the absence of facilities for such detailed research, is it not better to achieve what understanding we can rather than neglect it entirely? And in any case, I am not sure that the usual forms of empirical inquiry will necessarily bring to the surface some of the most interesting conclusions.

Authors of books on student revolt usually feel the need

for an *apologia*. There is a guilty awareness that too many books have already been written about it, and more than a suspicion that the reason for this is that academics are more interested in what goes on in their own back garden than in assessing events by some more universal criterion of importance. My own *apologia* is that, although student revolt in Britain is but a marginal aspect of our political affairs, it does throw an interesting light on certain more significant questions. Second, small though it is, the student movement has the capacity to cause considerable disruption in universities, and universities are valuable and delicate institutions in whose welfare we should be interested. Finally, certain aspects of the student movement are fascinating objects of study for their own sake.

POSTSCRIPT: STUDENT REVOLT 1969–70

Events that feature in the narrative of student revolt in Chapters Two to Four take us up to the end of the academic year 1968–69. In the subsequent year there were some developments of interest, and although it has not been possible to discuss these in detail the following brief summary attempts to locate them in the context of the analysis of this study.

Despite the premonitions and forecasts of most observers, the year began quietly. The major incidents of the Michaelmas term occurred towards the end of it and marked a continuation of a theme of the previous year: opposition to university involvement in South Africa and Rhodesia. The most important of these incidents were at the Universities of London and Birmingham, the institutions which had special relations with University College, Rhodesia. Although there were some bitter confrontations on this question, the issue eventually resolved itself when the universities ended the special relation following the declaration of a republic in Rhodesia.

One point which emerged from these confrontations was a new willingness by university authorities to take stern measures against protesters. This would seem to follow the pattern of the "third stage" of reaction to student revolt discussed in Chapter Five (p 139f). This feature remained true throughout the year, and the most outstanding example was at the London School of Economics. The authorities succeeded in having a student of the University of London, Paul Hoch, committed to prison for one month for refusing to give an undertaking not to continue breaking an injunction not to enter the School's premises.

Although this was the most severe form of action taken against a student, the extent of the protest against it within the college was small. Clear evidence of the failure of any mass campaign of protest to succeed was the existence of small anonymous groups committing acts of vandalism, the most serious of which was the destruction by fire of certain valuable manuscript maps owned by the geography department. The injunction on Hoch was part of the aftermath of the *fracas* at the School the previous year, which had itself seen a steep decline in the power of the student movement there.

Isolated acts of vandalism were a feature of some other protests during the year. Students at Essex tried to set fire to a campus branch of Barclays Bank, because of the involvement of Barclays DCO with South Africa, and at the end of the academic year a protest over disciplinary action at the University of Keele occasioned acts of violence, leading to the suspension of the county council's grant to the university.

But the most significant student protests of the year occurred in the Lent term at the University of Warwick, where students occupying a building in the course of a demonstration raided secret files in the office of the Vice-Chancellor. Some of the material found related to the question of University College, Rhodesia, and was used by students involved in that campaign. But more important was evidence that the university had received reports on students' political views from head teachers, and that similar information may have been used by the university when giving references to prospective employers. Further, there was evidence that officials of the American-owned motor manufacturers, the Rootes Group, had been objecting (without success) to the Vice-Chancellor about a member of the academic staff who had made speeches critical of private enterprise. The Rootes Group and other large companies have strong links with the University of Warwick, which has set a precedent in close industry-university relations. The discovery of these documents led to a wave of demands to "open the books" at several universities, and there were several sit-ins.

Although this particular theme of protest was novel it was well in keeping with certain existing preoccupations of the student left, and in fact the analysis of issues in the Conclusion to Chapter Four can readily accommodate it: paragraph iv (p 125) deals with concern at the relationship between the university and certain forces in the outside world. The issue of confidential files and the Rootes intervention relate to the same point. Thus although this major protest occurred too late to be included in the main body of this study, it confirms its major thesis.

ACKNOWLEDGEMENTS

I must acknowledge the enormous amount of assistance given to me by Miss Joan Freedman in collecting data and material, and in subsequent checking of drafts and proofs. I am also indebted to Mr Anthony Raven for his work on the Index.

Finally, I should thank the members, past and present, of the Socialist Society of the London School of Economics for having been such curious phenomena and intransigent opponents. Without the stimulus of trying to understand them I might never have taken so much interest in the student movement and its surrounding issues.

Colin Crouch
London School of Economics and Political Science
June 1970

PART ONE

A History of
Student Revolt in Britain

CHAPTER ONE

Political Orientations

If a revolutionary student in Britain is asked to say why he protests, why he uses direct action, why he is continually seeking new demonstrations and confrontations, he is likely to answer in terms that have very little to do with the university as such. He will tell how the working class in Britain has been betrayed by the hierarchy of the Labour Party, how genuinely democratic grass-roots activity is ruled out by the machinations of the political system, how Parliamentary and constitutional politics are not a valid weapon with which to combat the overweening power of capitalism and imperialism.

He may also tell how the movement for direct action has developed since the Campaign for Nuclear Disarmament made its first limping, liberal gestures towards the politics of the street, and how the idea has been developed from there to involve a theory of the use of direct action, the occupation of factories and universities, as the only relevant political activity at the present time.

Alternatively he may reach further back into history and discuss the fate of the proletarian revolutionary movement since Karl Marx attempted to give birth to it; how it has emerged in full democratic glory at certain moments of time: at the Paris Commune in 1870, after the Russian Revolution in 1917, possibly in China and Cuba, in France and Czechoslovakia in 1968; in each instance only to be crushed either by the powerful agencies of the capitalist state or betrayed by its own power-hungry bureaucracy; how the movement is still, despite all, eventually destined to succeed, to spread among the oppressed workers of the west, the east and the

15

third world, to usher in a glorious new dawn of freedom, of libertarian socialism. No sure blueprint may be provided for the progress of this revolution, for its development must rest with the workers to whom it belongs. Meanwhile, the student movement which has emerged may play its tiny part in building the movement and helping the workers.

A credo very much on these lines is likely to be given by any thoughtful student revolutionary in Britain called upon to state his political position and how he reached it. If the student is American, the pattern will be similar, with experience in the Civil Rights movement in the South replacing the Campaign for Nuclear Disarmament and with considerably less emphasis on Karl Marx. Although individual outbreaks of student protest can be related to specific proximate causes within a particular university, and although it is possible to indicate broader changes within educational institutions which lie behind student revolt, it is impossible to understand it properly without this wider political context. It is one of the main purposes of this book to show how and why the internal university situation and the wider political issues are inextricably linked. It is indeed the strength and number of these links that have given the student protest movement its tenacity and persistence. It is therefore necessary to begin an account of how student protest has developed in Britain with a brief discussion of the political context in which its participants have framed their perspectives.

Most student revolutionaries belong somewhere in that small and fragmented group known as the new left; a movement which has developed as totally alienated from and hostile to the mainstream of the British Labour movement. Although several of these groups started life in the early sixties or before, relationships with the orthodox Labour movement have, inevitably, soured during the period of Labour Government since 1964. When, in 1965, two prominent members of the new left – Robin Blackburn and Perry Anderson – edited a selection of essays[1] on socialism, they included among the contributors Richard Crossman, Lord (then Thomas) Balogh and Richard Titmuss. It is unlikely that these five men would now appear together in one volume.*

Although the new left sees as its major enemy the traditional trinity of capitalism, imperialism and reaction, in practice much of its deepest hatred and bitterest invective is reserved for the Parliamentary left and what has become known as "Establishment liberalism". In its selection of tactics in particular the new left often seems more concerned to prove a point to a past generation of left-wingers than to achieve a particular objective. We shall have opportunity to illustrate and expand this point at later stages; for the present it is sufficient to note this element of disillusion with a previous generation of radicals that is very important to the character of the student protest.

There is something of a deliberate gesture of frustration in several aspects of this revolt, something which says to the wider world "See what you have made me do". This is, of course, not a gesture of complete alienation; it is the gesture of those who feel they have been forced to take action of a certain kind because the political system does not live up to its own theory. In other words, the revolutionary may at times present himself as the only genuine advocate of values to which widespread lip-service is given. It is noteworthy that the leaders of protest groups are often the sons of liberal intellectuals of the previous generation. Similar observations have been made in a study by Kenneth Keniston of the leaders of a Vietnam protest movement. He discusses not only the prevalence of liberal middle-class parents among their origins, but also the commitment of the radicals to certain proclaimed values of American society. Their alienation results precisely from the apparent failure of the society to maintain these values:

". . . what is most impressive is not their secret motivation to have the system fail, but their naïve hope that it would

* In 1969 Blackburn was dismissed from LSE for his part in student revolt there. Another contributor to *Towards Socialism*, Tom Nairn, was lecturer at Hornsey College of Art at the time of the massive disturbances there in 1968.

succeed, and the extent of their depression and disillusion when their early reformist hopes were frustrated. . . . Although these radicals' fidelity to most of the creedal values of American society remained firm, their sense of connection to the institutions and practices of our society became attenuated."[2]

The general stance of the new left has thus tended to be that of the betrayed. In addition to this general mood it is possible to isolate certain events of recent history which have played a particularly important part in shaping their perspectives. Although political philosophies are couched in universal language, their contents are usually much influenced by major incidents which make specific aspects of politics particularly salient, or provide warnings and examples. To a large extent the new left feeds on similar historical material as the rest of the British left: the Russian revolution; the problems of the 1920s and 1930s; the betrayal of the Labour Party by its leadership in 1931; the rise of Hitler and fascism. But other, more particular, themes also appear in the conversation and literature.

THE PROBLEM OF SOVIET COMMUNISM

First, very considerable importance is placed on the invasion of Hungary by the Soviet Union in 1956. This very dramatic representation of the myth of the workers' democracy came early in the lives of most members of the new left, and thus their disillusion with the Soviet road to socialism occupies a more central and integrated place in their political framework than it did in that of the generation of left-wingers who experienced more directly the trauma of disillusion in "the god that failed". Distrust of state centralism and of the whole approach of using the modern state to achieve socialism from the top is very important to modern revolutionaries. The new left stands very firmly in the localist, community-oriented, near anarchist tradition of left-wing politics, in firm opposition to the other dominant theme – that of the strong centralised state. In this the new left contrast very strongly

18

with their immediate predecessors in the British far left. The contrast is perhaps even more important in those western European countries where communism has been strong. There the Communist Party has found itself completely out of touch with a movement which regards it as bureaucratic, undemocratic and, indeed, non-revolutionary. Of course, Hungary is by no means the sole explanation of this attitude of the new left towards the communist world. Hungary provided the dramatic event which made it possible to put the whole development of eastern European communism into a particular perspective. Daniel and Gabriel Cohn-Bendit, for example, claim to identify an alliance between the Communist Party in France and the bourgeoisie since the Popular Front in the 1930s. They are mainly interested in the relationship between the Communist "bureaucratic" trade-union leadership and the managerial class:

"... But not content with this subservient role, the 'workers' bureaucracy has been trying to wrest a seat in the very centres of economic power, on the boards of the increasingly important State industries, the latest offspring of the capitalist system ... their model of society – State, property, planning, specialist control of the economy, a social hierarchy based on ability, the subordination of man to the industrial machine, the improvement of living conditions through the production of more consumer goods, State control of all social and cultural activities – does not differ essentially from that of the economic bureaucracy."[3]

THE FATE OF SOCIAL DEMOCRACY

Second, there is the recent history of the social democratic parties of Britain and Europe in politics. In Britain the new left sees the Labour Party in power taking the concept of public ownership and draining it of its potential democratic implications, translating it into the depoliticised notion of nationalisation in the interests of rationalised production methods and greater economic efficiency. The role of the state, whatever the party in power, is seen as inherently

19

malevolent. In some ways the new left shows a less naïve approach to the problems of government in western democracies than its predecessors in the more orthodox Labour movement. It is more aware than they of the pressures that operate on governments from powerful institutions in the economy which are able to reduce or indeed obviate the difference in the direction of government that can be wrought by a change in political control at a general election.

The central doctrines of Socialism, it is argued, have been adapted by the Labour establishment to the modern technological economy, where capitalism maintains its dominance, not through the operation of the market, but through a coalition with the state to manage an increasingly *dirigist* economy; the powers of government are enlisted to ensure the obedience of a population whose aspirations will not conflict with the smooth operation of the economic machine. If a single policy can be said to symbolise this development that the new left sees in modern social democracy, it is the incomes policy. Surrounded as it is by a rhetoric of socialism in the language of Government spokesmen (planned, orderly growth of incomes; restraint in the interest of low-paid workers, and so forth) it is seen as having the real purpose of suppressing agitation by workers against their employers:

"... the units of capitalism are now so large and their investments are now so complex that the capitalists have, however reluctantly, had to accept the idea of planning and co-ordination by the state. As other countries have entered the world market, and Britain's share in the world market has continued to decline, international competition has in many ways replaced competition in the local British market, and there has been increasing concern with 'national interest' – the interests of British capitalism as a whole – an interest that only the state can properly define and push. So the state today, through NEDDY, the Department of Economic Affairs, the Prices and Incomes Board, and the many other state planning and coordinating agencies, seeks to do British capitalism's planning job.

This it does, of course, on the capitalists' own terms, and wherever possible it draws in businessmen to help the civil servants. The state and business thus have become much more highly integrated today. Politics and economics can hardly be separated any more. And it is difficult to see the state as 'neutral' outside the conflict between the classes. Tory or Labour, it makes less and less difference: the Government of today is much more clearly a government of the employers, for the employers and by the employers. This is only emphasised by the declining power of Parliament in relation to the Cabinet and the government departments. What good is there in pinning all your hopes on a bunch of Labour MPs who can do nothing anyway, because they are powerless?"[4]

A wide and instructive contrast exists between this attitude to recent extensions of Government economic intervention and the attitudes of the Bevanites, when state action in the hands of a Labour Government was seen as an extension of popular democratic power. It is this experience which contributes towards several very important characteristics of the new left: first, their complete disaffection from Parliamentary and ballot-box politics, which leads to their advocacy of direct action, the politics of the street and other elements of deliberately non-constitutional protest. Second, there is a total cynicism towards all conventional political debate. Third, these developments in the British Labour Party* are seen as running closely parallel to the developments in the USSR that we discussed above. In both cases it is alleged that the slogans of socialism and state control have been twisted out of their democratic context and used to provide the state with a ready means of manipulating the populace

---

* Similar processes were to be observed in the USA (with the apparent inability of the Democratic Johnson regime to follow policies on Vietnam significantly different from those advocated by Senator Goldwater); in West Germany (following the decision of the Social Democratic Party to join a coalition with the Christian Democrats); and in France (with the general enervation of politics under de Gaulle).

in the interests of the rulers of the industrial structure. This theme has been elaborated in some detail by a prominent American radical (and veteran of Berkeley), who takes the process back beyond the immediate experience of the 1964 Labour Government. He seeks to explain the enthusiastic response of the Webbs, the founders of British Fabianism, to Stalin's Russia in the 1930s:

". . . While Fabianism as a special tendency petered out into the larger stream of Labour Party reformism by 1918, the leading Fabians themselves went in another direction. Both Sidney and Beatrice Webb as well as Bernard Shaw – the top trio – became principled supporters of Stalinist totalitarianism in the 1930s. Even earlier, Shaw, who thought socialism needed a Superman, had found more than one. In turn he embraced Mussolini and Hitler. . . . In 1931 Shaw disclosed, after a visit to Russia, that the Stalin regime was really Fabianism in practice. The Webbs followed to Moscow, and found God. . . .

"They staunchly supported Stalin through the Moscow purge trials and the Stalin-Hitler Pact without a visible qualm, and died more uncritical pro-Stalinists than can now be found on the Politburo. As Shaw himself explained, the Webbs had nothing but scorn for the Russian Revolution itself, but 'The Webbs waited until the wreckage and ruin of the change was ended, its mistakes remedied, and the Communist State fairly launched.' That is, they waited until the revolutionary masses had been straitjacketed, the leaders of the revolution cashiered, the efficient tranquility of dictatorship had settled on the scene, the counter-revolution firmly established; and then they came along to pronounce it the Ideal.

"Was this really a gigantic misunderstanding, some incomprehensible blunder? Or were they not right in thinking that this indeed was the 'socialism' that matched their ideology, give or take a little blood? The swing of Fabianism from middle-class permeation to Stalinism was the swing of a door that was hinged on Socialism-from-Above."[5]

GUERRILLAS AND CULTURAL REVOLUTION

The third influence on the new left of considerable importance has been the experience of Cuba, the Chinese cultural
revolution and the Vietnam war. Both Cuba and China
provide the model of cultural revolution, which is seen as
providing an alternative "democratic" model to the political
revolution from the top exemplified by the Soviet Union.
Cultural revolution implies (whatever the reality in the countries concerned may be) action throughout the whole society,
with the emphasis on changes in the everyday lives of the
ordinary people. It means workers taking control of their
own lives, expanding their consciences and horizons beyond
the narrow limits that had been permitted by exploitative
regimes. The concept is seen as potentially as meaningful to
the worker in the mass-production factory of disciplined
western industry as to the peasant working in paddy fields or
plantations.

This model of revolution is preferred on both moral and
intellectual grounds to the idea of purely political revolution. Morally, it is considered essential that the workers
participate in the revolution directly, in their own life experience, and do not give up this responsibility to a centralised élite. Intellectually, it is considered that a revolution
cannot be thorough-going unless the break with the previous
way of life is complete.*

The Cuban revolution, and more important the Vietnam
war, have a further significance in that they provide the
immensely important model of guerrilla warfare. The Vietnam war is, of course, to many on the left terrifying evidence
of the cruelty and immorality of the society which has been
held up to them as the example of civilised life. For Americans, who have the additional problem of the draft to make
the issue of more than theoretical importance to them, the

---

* In some ways this idea is not as new as it is frequently claimed to
be; very similar ideas were strong in the early days of the Russian and
French revolutions, an important example in the latter being the change
in the calendar that was temporarily introduced. This and similar reforms were intended to embody the spirit of rationalism.

war, together with the race issue, is the major cause of their disaffection from their parent society. But the guerrilla model has a further importance. The guerrilla band is a small face-to-face group. It is, at least in the eyes of romantic young revolutionaries, voluntaristic, autonomous, non-bureaucratic. The fighters are seen as working passionately for a cause in which they believe *and* which represents their own best ideal and material interests. The guerrilla is thus virtually the ideal type of non-alienated man. It is through such an interpretation of guerrilla warfare that the revolutionary student in a western university is able to identify himself with the jungle warrior.

But the attraction of the guerrilla goes further. Not only does he himself conform to the ideal picture of revolutionary man, but in Vietnam guerrilla bands have been able to tie down, perhaps yet to beat, the most technologically equipped and bureaucratically co-ordinated army the world has ever seen. This fact, which can no doubt be explained in terms of geographical and logistical factors, is imbued with profound significance by the new left. So rich in symbolism is the Vietnam war that it acquires the status of the struggles of the beasts of the Apocalypse. For the new left a victory for the Vietcong would represent a victory for all their aspirations against everything they loathe. It is not surprising that slogans about Vietnam intrude into every demonstration held, or that demonstrations over Vietnam have been able to muster, even in this country, which is not directly involved, vaster support than those on Rhodesia, Biafra or incomes policy.

Robin Blackburn has presented an elaboration of this view which, significantly, finds its point of departure in an attack on Max Weber's concept of rational bureaucratic organisation and his assertion that it is technically the most superior devised by man:*

* It will be noted that Weber's own profound pessimism at the development of bureaucratic rationality is conveniently ignored, if not belied, by this account. This true of the whole essay from which the quotation is a short excerpt.

"For Weber, the modern bureaucratic army was a prime instance of the superior power and 'rationality' of this form of organisation. Indeed the whole development of his theory reflects the impression made on him by the apparent success of Prussian military bureaucracy. Yet the history of this century shows that bureaucratized armies can be defeated by guerrilla armies. Today the highly bureaucratized armed forces of the largest imperial power in the world have shown their impotence when faced with an authentic popular army. Every guerrilla army of this sort violates the commands of Weber's superior rationality."[6]

ALIENATION

Fourth, the new left, like all other political groups, has had to respond to the growth in affluence that has happened since the second world war and the important effect this has had on perception of class inequalities. Partly the new left's approach to this has been to point out that the change in overall prosperity has occurred with hardly any change in the relative distribution of wealth; but other writers on the more orthodox left have also adopted this position, and it is not particularly distinctive of the new left. More important where they are concerned is the shift of emphasis from physical deprivations and inequalities to inequalities of participation and involvement in work, and inequalities of power and control at work. The development of these ideas has been facilitated by the fact that those industries in which prosperous manual workers have emerged have often been those with the most "alienating" work environment – the mass-production assembly-line industries of which the motor industry is the prime example.

This point of reference, which is shared with several other researchers[7] not at all connected with the new left, is but the launching point for a general theory of alienation which goes far beyond the conditions of certain modern industries to embrace the whole of modern employment. We are now in

25

the centre of the new left's most sacred texts: the early writings of Marx[8] on alienated labour. Man is here seen as essentially a worker: ideally man fulfils himself and realises his vocation by extending himself in the meaningful creation of things; in such work, man's personality is actively engaged, and he exercises control over, and autonomy in, what he does and how he does it. This is contrasted with work under capitalism. Here man's work is carried on under the control of employers and supervisors who rob him of his autonomy, dictate what he is to do and how to do it. The whole system is guided and governed by the operation of the market; an impersonal, non-human force which sets an impregnable barrier – money – between a man's personality and his work. Man is thus robbed of both meaningfulness and control.

Obviously an analysis of this scope is not to be restricted to such obvious cases as the motor industry. Even in crafts where men *feel* they are engaged and involved in their labours, this is carried on under a capitalist system and they are therefore suffering from an illusion of meaningfulness. Indeed, in some analyses even the capitalist is considered as alienated, for he also has to accept the dictates of the market:

> "In this sense, according to Marx, 'The possessing class and the proletarian class express the same human alienation. But the former is satisfied with its situation, feels itself well established in it, recognizes this self-alienation as its own power and thus has the *appearance* of a human existence' (1844 Manuscripts). The essential alienation of capitalist society is that it is presided over not by man, but by the market."[9]

The idea of alienation is thus of great use. Whatever changes may take place in material prosperity and physical oppression, a deprivation defined so totally will continue to exist. The idea also has its roots in certain experiences of modern society. We have commented on the question of modern industry; there is also the matter of bureaucracy, which has been emerging as a twin alongside capitalism in

Marxist demonology ever since Trotsky's early apprehensions about the role of the state in post-revolutionary Russia. It is of the essence of bureaucracy that the individuals occupying certain roles divest themselves of personal interest and involvement in their role, and act according to the dictates of functional rationality in carrying out the tasks of the organisation. Obviously, in terms of the Marxist concept of alienated labour, this whole class of occupations stands condemned. Finally, this point relates back to the question of the disillusion with politics as a meaningless and powerless activity, and to the concept of cultural revolution as a fulfilling and non-alienated activity, as it engages man in his totality.

The opposite of alienation is "meaningful participation": the idea of an engagement in society and its affairs that is both personally satisfying and politically powerful. In this way participation has emerged as a major plank in the new left's programme, and in the particular case of student revolt it has appeared as the key issue. It is also perhaps the issue raised by the new left which has passed most successfully into the rhetoric of conventional politics, from General de Gaulle to the Ministry of Housing and Local Government's committee on Participation in Planning. Needless to say, in the course of this transfer the idea of participation has become distinctly less exotic.

RACE

A fifth important formative influence is less easy to accommodate to the others, which mutually reinforce and feed each other. However, since it has been so important in recent fringe-group politics it would be wrong to omit it in the interests of a neat argument and concise theory. This is the issue of race, which has appeared in many different forms. Some aspects, such as the strengthening of immigration control by a Labour Government and the failure to take strong action against Rhodesia, have helped confirm the disillusion felt with the Labour Party.

27

In the USA an extremely important factor in creating the revolutionary student movement – indeed, the originating factor – was the Civil Rights movement in the southern states and its experience of the hostility of white society, police violence and the murder of civil rights workers condoned, or even connived at, by the local representatives of law and order.* Further, the whole problem of the increasing relative poverty of the third world and the increasing reluctance of the advanced countries to offer anything beyond minimal assistance is a strong source of disaffection from their own societies felt by members of the new left, providing them with alliances of fellow-feeling against their own society with peoples from very different and distant cultures.

But the race issue has more uncomfortable implications for the left as well. The tendency for militant negro movements to become racialist themselves has led, in the USA, to the almost complete inability of the revolutionary student movement to work with the black student movement. In Britain, Marxists find extremely depressing a movement towards black power that appears to have revolutionary potential, but which finds its rallying point in race rather than class.

Meanwhile, even more discomfiture is caused by the tendency of a proportion of white workers to give support to racialist agitation. When dockers marched in London in support of Mr Enoch Powell after he had made his first inflammatory speech on the question of coloured people in Britain, the student left was thrown into considerable confusion. Here was, of all things, a group of workers marching in support of a political cause, showing the desire to break free of existing political structures dreamed of by the left, but doing so in support of a right-wing Conservative speaking on the issue of race.

The problem has tended to be resolved by seeing the sup-

---

* It is difficult to over-emphasise the impact on sensitive, intelligent, middle-class young northerners of these murders. It has left its indelible mark of disaffection, estrangement and cynicism on the attitude of many such young Americans towards the society of their parents. There has been no comparable experience in this country.

port of racialist agitation as indicating frustration with the political consensus, an increasing willingness of groups of workers to enter the necessary preliminary stages of revolutionary activity; the only problem is that, at present, the unrest is being manipulated by the agents of false consciousness and diverted into channels useful to them. If only this can be broken down, the argument continues, there will be a great opportunity for the revolutionary left to rescue a vital workers' movement from the impending wreck of the British political system, as it grinds to a halt through the exhaustion of spurious debate in a stifling consensus. Thus the main impact of the race issue has been to heighten the revolutionary's sense of urgency and impending success, a vital attribute of any revolutionary movement if it is to retain and grow in strength in the face of apparently overwhelming odds.

FROM CND TO STUDENT REVOLT

Finally, one needs to bear in mind the political experience of the new left itself since its emergence through CND in the fifties.

Although it always attracted a large number from the far-left political margin, CND was in many ways an instance of constitutional and non-revolutionary political action. This was not often realised at the time by the press and other spokesmen, but it is amusing to note how, after the violent demonstrations in Grosvenor Square in 1968, CND's peacefulness was invoked with something approaching nostalgia by precisely those organs which had attacked it in its heyday.

CND tried, initially, to change the policies of the Labour Party by working through its channels. At the same time it used the techniques of direct action, but in the form of passive demonstrations and deliberate non-violence. The effect on the political system appeared negligible. At the same time, the experience of the Civil Rights movement in the USA was making itself felt. There direct action had been used in a more forceful way to achieve objectives. It had been used as a direct tactical weapon, rather than as a moral witness or as symbolic pressure. The new left began to re-appraise its attitude towards CND, and its conclusions have been tersely summarised by Gareth Stedman-Jones:

"(CND) remained as it had begun, an expression of the liberal tradition of British political culture, more comparable to the Campaign against the Boer War than to the SDS in Berlin or the Provos in Amsterdam. It encapsulated the hallmarks of radical liberalism – great idealism, intellectual confusion, and a virtual absence of strategy or tactics. True to its ancestry, it relied upon the appeal to men of good will. . . . A second legacy of CND was an incomprehension of the necessity of violence in certain political circumstances. CND was inspired by the non-violent dissent of Gandhi; it thereby mistook a tactic for a principle."[10]

CONCLUSION

If we may conflate the effect of these six major sources of influence on the new left, we find a movement which has rejected the Soviet path to a bureaucratic socialism, and which sees Western social democracy as having succumbed to the influence of capitalist society to the extent that it, like Soviet Communism, no longer represents the interests of the proletariat but those of the class-ruled technocratic state. The politics of the ballot box is a mirage, because in existing society no change is possible that could represent a real alternative; change will only become possible once the great edifice of vested interests that rule men's lives and deny them their freedom has crashed for all time. The impossibility of politics and the control of economic life by a ruling class is reflected in the impossibility of true human freedom. Men are alienated from their work in that all they may do is perform some small task in a grand structure whose design is completely beyond their control. In this way society systematically robs man of his scope for action. The assembly line serves as a model for all life and all institutions.

Finally, this class society is seen as exploiting racialism both abroad in the form of colonialism and neo-colonialism and at home in the form of hostile policies towards black racial minorities. This is seen as finally compounding the corruption of existing society, and relating it directly with the fascist systems that terrorised the world in the 1930s.

In stark contrast to this bleak image stands the guerrilla and the cultural revolution, strengthened by the left's own experience of political protest. A revolution is required, and it must be a revolution of a particular type. It must not accept the constraints imposed upon action by the world. It must not allow itself to be enervated in its revolutionary force by forms, structures or bureaucracies. It must in itself be an instance of the transcendence of alienation. It must therefore be participative, egalitarian, unrestrained by the sterile confinements of rationality and political appropriateness. Revolutionary action must begin now. It must strike at as many institutions of existing society as possible; and the form of the revolution must be mass-participative direct action at the grass roots.

These were the political attitudes that had been reached by many young people of the left in the mid-1960s. They were the attitudes with which they came to university, or they were attitudes which have developed while they were there. By now, of course, new university entrants are predominantly people whose early experience has been somewhat different from the original agitators of the movement. These young men and women have spent their adolescence in a period of Labour Government; they do not even need to experience disillusion, but come with attitudes that slip easily into the forms of the new left. They have also completed their school years at a time when student revolt has already become a much-publicised part of politics. Thus if the new entrants lack the political experiences that shaped some of the original character of the student revolt movement, they compensate by frequently arriving at the university as ready and willing protesters.

31

REFERENCES

1. Anderson, P. and Blackburn, R. (eds), *Towards Socialism*, 1965
2. Keniston, K., *Young Radicals*, 1968, pp 127, 130
3. Cohn-Bendit, D. and G., *Obsolete Communism: The Left-Wing Alternative*, 1968, pp 170–1
4. Cliff, T. and Barker, C., *Incomes Policy, Legislation and Shop Stewards*, 1966, p 127
5. Draper, H., *The Two Souls of Socialism*, 1966, p 16
6. Blackburn, R., "A Brief Guide to Bourgeois Ideology" (in Cockburn, A. and Blackburn, R. (eds), *Student Power*, 1969, p 181
7. e.g., Blauner, R., *Alienation and Freedom*, 1964; Chinoy, E., *Automobile Workers and the American Dream*, 1955
8. Marx, K., *Economic and Philosophical Manuscripts*, 1844 (for a useful analysis of these aspects of Marx, see Tucker, R., *Philosophy and Myth in Karl Marx*, 1961)
9. Blackburn, R., "The New Capitalism" (in Anderson and Blackburn, *op cit*). (Blackburn returns to similar themes in "A Brief Guide to Bourgeois Ideology", *op cit*)
10. Stedman-Jones, G., "The Meaning of Student Revolt" (in Cockburn and Blackburn, *op cit*) pp 43, 44

CHAPTER TWO

Student Revolt at LSE, 1965–67

A reputation for being "left wing" was acquired by the London School of Economics and Political Science in the 1930s and 1940s when Harold Laski, R. H. Tawney and other prominent figures of the intellectual left taught there. It lingered on for years after the character of its teaching body had changed very much in a right-ward direction. This LSE reputation is about the only element of continuing "tradition" in the British student movement, in great contrast with France and some other countries. A certain number of those students who went to the LSE in the period after the re-election of Labour in 1964 did so in the hope of finding some kind of political activity on the left among the student body.

By October 1965 Labour had been in office for twelve months, which was long enough for angry disillusion to be the predominant mood on the far left. The Labour Society, the strongest political society at that time in the college, had just suffered the latest in a series of splits spread over several decades, and a Socialist Society on Marxist-Trotskyist lines had been established. This society contained within it a small group of highly articulate and intensely passionate ideologues who were fired with a pentecostal urge to convert and proselytise. They would come to meetings of the Labour Society, which were usually addressed by Labour MPs, to relate how Labour had betrayed the working class and sold out to capitalism. They would, if one showed a glimmering of interest, buttonhole one in the bar or a public house and relate how the politics of "four per cent growth rates"*

* It will be recalled that this was a recurrent theme of the Labour Party before and after the 1964 election, lasting until the collapse of the National Plan.

33

ignored the basic conflicts of class in society and could not possibly raise man from the inevitable alienation of the capitalist system. They tried, with some success, to make contact with shop stewards and various unofficial workers' representatives. They arranged an impressive series of meetings, attracting speakers of the status of Deutscher.

But all this was mainly evident only to those of us generally on the left, who attended meetings and involved ourselves in political discussions. In the students' union, where a wider cross-section of political views was to be found, they had less influence. The prevailing ethos of the students' union at that time was a vague Labourism, a heavy pre-occupation with little internal union scandals, all touched with a humour ranging from sardonic wit to childishness. It was not an atmosphere in which spokesmen of a hard Marxist line could uncompromisingly hold sway, as was later to be the case. In any case, the Marxists were not very interested in student politics; they usually participated in the union only when wider political issues were being discussed.

The wider issue that occupied us most during that year was, significantly, Rhodesia. The unilateral declaration of independence had been made in November and we had our first taste of a student demonstration by marching to Rhodesia House, which was conveniently situated at the other end of the Strand; there were arrests. The Rhodesian issue was of course not the private property of the Marxists; a wide consensus of political instincts could be appealed to, especially in a college with a large percentage of African students. At that time the left-wing position on Rhodesia was in any case to call for the intervention of the British Army. However, although the far left could not dominate and impose their specific philosophy on the demonstrations, in the course of the actual protest they would come to the fore; they would arrive with the banners, take the lead on the march, and, as likely as not, be arrested. Within the debating hall, in discussion, the Socialist Society did not have an atmosphere it could dominate; it was in action that they found their milieu.

Although Rhodesia and race were the only issues which

appeared likely to arouse the student body to mass action, some of us, in addition to those on the far left, hoped to explore further possibilities. Important in this was the fact that David Adelstein, an early advocate of student power and a firm believer in mass participative democracy, had become president of the students' union in February 1966. He had seen the possibilities for students to press for greater involvement in the running of universities.

Our interest in achieving this participation was based to a large extent on irritation at the apparent imperviousness and impersonality of LSE's administrative apparatus. Frustrations were intensified rather than assuaged by membership of the staff-student committee, of which I was a member in 1966. No, we would be told at each meeting, this committee could not really discuss substantive student complaints; even less possible was the hope of securing personal support or sympathy from the staff members of the committee. They saw their task as being simply a post-box; telling us where we should go with complaints if we had any, but going no further than that. The most revolutionary proposal to emerge from the staff-student committee was that a circular of information should be prepared by the administration and made available to students, telling them what matters were being considered by various committees in the school; the idea was found to be impracticable.*

These frustrations were supplemented by a wider, vaguer, ideological position that believed in democracy and mass participation as of right. Along with others, I considered that an essential element of equality was democratic participation. We hoped to see such participation within the student body, but had recognised that mass interest could only be achieved in the event of a "big issue", such as Rhodesian UDI had been. Towards the end of the academic year 1965–66 we therefore resolved that a demand for greater student participation in the running of LSE should be launched as a major campaign the following October. Adelstein set two groups to

* It has now been implemented in truncated form (November 1969).

35

work; one group prepared a policy on representation and the other (of which I was a member) prepared a set of tactics for direct action by students to achieve implementation of these demands if we did not receive a favourable response. I recall that we did not consider it feasible to include a general student sit-in on the Berkeley model as part of our policy of direct action. The final stage of escalation we envisaged was disruption of the library. (In retrospect and after experience of several student protests, it seems that this idea, if implemented, would have been more serious and disruptive than a general sit-in.)

So plans had been laid that would, if successful, create an on-going protest of greater significance than the demonstrations we had planned earlier that year. Student politics would be raised to a more serious level than had traditionally been the case, and the whole thing seemed to be oriented towards worth-while ends. The Socialist Society had only been involved marginally in these plans. They were not very interested in the student situation as such; also, Adelstein and the rest of the moderate left were somewhat suspicious of them as being politically unstable, while they suspected us as student politicians.

MICHAELMAS TERM, 1966

During the summer, however, members of the Socialist Society had also been working on some plans for the new year. Dr (now Sir) Walter Adams, principal of University College, Rhodesia, had been appointed director of LSE. During the summer term of 1966 the Socialist Society had shown a passing, but not serious, interest in the issue of a new director by running a mock (and most unsuccessful) election for director in their magazine "Agitator". But now that the Rhodesian issue had appeared, they took a new interest. Throughout the summer two* of their number had worked

* For some reason the pamphlet itself claimed to be the product of the labours of about twenty students.

36

to produce a pamphlet: "LSE's new director: a report on Walter Adams", which attempted to demonstrate, through the judicious manipulation of excerpts from certain reports on UCR, that Dr Adams had shown unwillingness to defend academic freedom, had avoided important decision-making, had been extremely isolated from both academic staff and students, and (strange though such a complaint was, coming from a left-wing source) had been guilty of certain administrative inefficiencies. The pamphlet appeared in the third week of term, and attracted immediate interest.[1]

It is noteworthy that this galvanising issue of British student revolt was very much linked to wider political concerns – the issue of Rhodesia which had appeared in our demonstrations of the previous year. It is also significant that the issue gained strength through showing a connection between these wider political questions and our own situation in the college. This has often been the case in student protest. One of the frustrations of student politics before the current wave of protests had been its impotence. One's protests could never affect anything. The impotence of this student politics is well summarised by Bernard Crick, who, I suspect, had the LSE union of the early sixties in mind when he wrote:

"Student politics is the politics of affirmation. Groups must be got, typically student groups themselves, to affirm certain principles or 'their stand' on each and every great issue of the day. If necessary, groups must be invented to do just this. Such a process of affirmation is quite endless. A judgement has to be delivered on everything of any conceivable importance . . . and all this usually goes with a complete forgetfulness that such politics is not really politics at all. Their attitude to political involvement is like that of the coy maid of the story towards marriage; they dart between fears too deep and hopes too high. There is almost nothing that can do less harm or good to man or beast, or which has less political power, than students' politics. They can, indeed, occasionally pass from affirmation to demonstration, thus setting some real problems for the

37

police and striving desperately – almost as an end in itself – 'to catch the public eye', that is, to get a paragraph in an evening paper. The making of gestures becomes an end in itself."[2]

Such had it been with us over Rhodesia. But now we had on our own doorstep an opportunity to become engaged in real politics; to do more than make a symbolic stand. If we could force Adams to withdraw as director of LSE we would actually have done something. The importance of this meant that the actual facts about what Dr Adams had done in Rhodesia, and our ability to pass judgement on him with so little information and experience of the situation there, became somewhat irrelevant. There were many doubts about the charges made in the Agitator pamphlet, but as the time for decision on the matter grew near it became clear that those who were passionately concerned about Rhodesia would support the criticisms of Adams, while the small number of students who were sympathetic to the Smith regime would oppose them.

There is a further point of general importance in understanding student revolt which was relevant to the wide acceptance given to the Agitator pamphlet. The major defence that could be made of Dr Adams's decision to remain at UCR despite UDI was that it might be in the best interests of a future multi-racial Rhodesia to keep alive the idea of multi-racialism in the college and to preserve the college as an island of freedom. (Whether or not this was the wisest course in the circumstances is a separate question; the point here is that such a position may be considered morally defensible.) But this was precisely the kind of argument which would fail to appeal to young people appearing on the new left. As suggested in the previous chapter, their protest is as much against the habits and approaches of a former generation of liberals as against such enemies as capitalism and racialism. Arguments based on the most effective means of achieving certain ends, and on the need to subjugate the desire to adopt idealistic postures in the interests of achieving practical long-term goals, were precisely the kinds of argument that would fail to appeal to them. Were not these the arguments with which the leaders of social democracy had compromised the interests of the working class in every country where they had come to power? Was not this the twisted approach of a devious, amoral politics that had to be fought and rejected?

The politics of the new left is the politics of instant moral affirmation. In their eyes it is better to fail disastrously through taking an uncompromising stand, than to achieve some of one's aims through taking part in the conventional process.

This moral stance provides a neat dovetailing of three different elements in the political mood that has come to predominate among groups of revolutionary students. First is the general contempt for what is seen as the hypocrisy of liberal politics. Second is the influence of existential philosophy and its demand that action be true to one's ultimate values, rejecting action that is justified by an appeal to the constraints of the situation or the obligations of a role. Third, the appeal of the revolutionary group, its claim to legitimacy and its ability to mobilise active support, are all based on its skill in making such direct and unambiguous stands itself. I have already mentioned in connection with the early stirrings of demonstrations that the revolutionaries needed a certain atmosphere before they could come into their own; we shall encounter the same point at frequent intervals.

Thus from early on the LSE affair can be seen as a clash between the new radicalism and the old liberalism, rather than the direct conflict between left and right that might be suggested by a superficial knowledge that Rhodesia was involved.

Nevertheless, the LSE students' union was not quite ready to pass judgement on the Adams question. A meeting was called on the issue and was attended by a record number of students (about 600). It refused to support a motion calling for the condemnation of the Adams appointment, and adopted a "moderate" (but futile) one proposed by another student and myself "seriously questioning" the appointment and calling for a reply to the criticisms within three weeks by Dr Adams. This amendment represented a genuine desire to

39

have more information before making a final judgement, but in fact it also struck a potentially radical attitude in its assumption that students had a right to question and examine the behaviour of the director-designate of their college. Although the Adams issue had knocked our summer plans for an offensive on student representation into the shade, as the term progressed they were to become united in a general demand for students to have a share in decision-making at major levels. The expression "student power" began to be used and take on some meaning.

But more immediately after the union's vote to question Adams's appointment our attention was drawn away by the intervention of new issues – the Court of Governors, disciplinary action and freedom of speech. The late Lord Bridges, chairman of the Court, decided that it was time to reply to the criticisms being made of Adams through a letter in *The Times*[3]. The union council considered that this letter called for a reply from the union, which was duly drafted. This in itself represented no great difficulty; Adelstein could write as a private individual and the letter could be published with no repercussions from the LSE authorities. However, should he reply as president of the LSE he would fall foul of a School regulation, which at that time forbade students to write to the press under the School's name.* Adelstein himself did not want to do this, as he did not particularly wish to be disciplined. Some others took the view that if Adelstein did not want to be disciplined it was not our job to force him to be so; but the Socialist Society, whose leading members had become more interested in the students' union as a result of the slowly escalating protest, thought otherwise. A stand needed to be taken; Adelstein as an elected representative should be subject to the will of the union and do as it bade him. In any case, why take steps which would avoid a confrontation with the authorities? An attempt was made to reconcile the two

* The origins of this prohibition lie in the troubles of LSE at an earlier period. The question is discussed at some length in *The Trouble at LSE*, by Harry Kidd,[4] a work to which considerable reference will be made in the course of the chapter.

sides before the union meeting that was scheduled to decide the matter, but it did not succeed. At the meeting itself the far left carried the day by a fair-sized majority, but I do not consider that this refutes my thesis that at this time the Socialist Society was still but an element, and by no means the predominant one, within a wider movement. The debate was swayed, not by the exhortation to confrontation, but by the intervention of two academics from the law department, who produced a tortuous argument to show that the proposed action was not, in fact, prohibited under the regulations.[5]

The letter was sent to *The Times*[6] and Adelstein discussed the position at length with the director, Sir Sidney Caine (relations between administration and students' union could still not be described as strained, let alone hostile). The director was courteous but correct, and it seemed inevitable that disciplinary action would follow. A group of students set about collecting 1,250 signatures on a petition saying that the decision to write to *The Times* had been the responsibility of the union as a whole, and not just Adelstein.

We were now aware that something like the student protest movement that we had sought was beginning to grow. It was growing untidily, sprawling over a range of issues. It included Adams's appointment, which itself included two issues – that of Rhodesia and that of student participation – and it also included the general question of student representation, which had by now been raised in the union. Now the intervention of the Court of Governors through (i) *The Times* letter from its chairman, and (ii) the impending role of the standing committee of the court in the disciplinary action, had introduced three explosive new elements.

First, the Bridges letter made it possible to see the court, not as a neutral arbiter of the School's destiny, but as having a political stance that could be hostile to the student movement; this strengthened demands for student representation in college government.

Second, the fact that a large proportion of the court consisted of representatives of British industry and finance meant that the devil himself had been formally added to the *dramatis personae*; the Socialist Society's theory of conspiratorial class rule could be, and was, applied to the government of the LSE as well as to the fate of the Labour Party in national government.

Finally, disciplinary action for, of all things, writing a letter to *The Times* – a letter written in reply to one from those persons instituting the disciplinary action – aroused a broad canvas of liberal opinion, and also introduced the issue of free speech which had been the *cause célèbre* at Berkeley.

Just as the issues were confused, there were differences among the various factions in the student body. As mentioned before, the Socialist Society by no means had control. They were prodding and goading, attempting to give a lead and coherence to the movement, but they were not sufficiently strong. Their language was strange and unfamiliar to the bulk of students; their political perspective, which was very much rooted in the developments discussed in the previous chapter, was not yet shared by many of their contemporaries. And the context within which the whole dispute was being conducted was cast in far too conventional a mould for their particular style and *élan* to gain impetus.

Possibly more successful were those of us who had best be described as the "moderates".* We did speak in a familiar language and probably shared the mood of a wider range of students. But we were by no means in control of events; we, like everyone else, were being tossed from issue to issue as the different events swept through the college. Meanwhile, the bulk support that was giving the movement strength at extremely well attended union meetings was also diffused. Many people were outraged by such actions as discipline for writing a letter; others were irritated by the LSE bureaucracy; others still maintained a primary interest in the Rhodesia issue.

---

* The term "moderate", which originally seemed to denote those students who sought certain radical ends but urged discretion in the adoption of direct action, has come subsequently to mean any student who opposes left-wing militants, however extremely that opposition is manifested.

Much is often made in analyses of student discontent of the lack of physical amenities, overcrowding in the library* and elsewhere, at LSE. These can be greatly exaggerated in importance. If physical deprivation were a major cause of student revolt, the protest would have occurred in the technical colleges, and in virtually no universities. Nevertheless, if physical conditions are difficult, as they undoubtedly were at the LSE, there will be a general irritability and dissatisfaction with the provision being made by the authorities. As a result authorities will have few reserves of loyalty within the student body to which they can appeal in times of crisis. To that extent alone physical conditions can be important.

Meanwhile, as may be expected, the majority of LSE students remained disinterested in the whole affair; this fact is often stressed by opponents of the student movement, although much the same criticism could be used to discredit virtually any government or authority in the world.

Those of us intimately involved in trying to steer the protest felt the need for a more vigorous flexing of muscles if we were to achieve anything on our increasingly broad span of issues. We decided to call on the union to support a one-day boycott of classes and lectures in protest against the authorities' stance on all our causes for complaint. A motion listing the authorities' offences and calling for the boycott was proposed to the union by myself and seconded by one of the leading members of the Socialist Society, Richard Kuper, a graduate student. We were defeated. The union was not ready for this kind of action; nothing had come to a head, and the average student could not be expected to take some form of direct protest on issues that were for him still academic. The revolutionaries, in their desire to see a full-scale protest in operation, were out of touch with the prevailing mood. For my part, I had seen some form of direct action as a necessary baring of teeth if the school authorities were to be encouraged to treat us with anything like the respect that

* In fairness to the LSE's reputation, it should be pointed out that since extensions were made to the library two years ago, it has not been overcrowded (October 1969).

43

opponents with some power base can usually command. But only those of us who had been actively involved in discussion and negotiation with the School authorities were likely to see matters in this light.

But within a couple of weeks the authorities acted by bringing the charges against Adelstein, and by organising his "trial" on lines that appeared to us to omit certain elements of that strange concept "natural justice". Again the union met, and this time a boycott was agreed and fixed to coincide with the date of the trial. At this time a boycott of lectures and classes appeared quite a radical step; in retrospect it was really very little. But several points are revealed by the set of incidents. The students' union, though representing that minority of students most interested in the political aspect of university life, was reluctant to take direct action on such a generalised issue. Still less were they prepared to act in response to a call from the revolutionaries. Like most British liberals, their hackles were only roused by what seemed to be an act of injustice against an individual, one of their colleagues.

It is therefore likely that in the absence of the authorities' disciplinary action it would not have been possible to set in motion a wide-scale active student protest movement at LSE. But, on the other hand, it is also striking that when authority did act, it found itself in a changed student environment from that to which it had become accustomed over the years. As Harry Kidd[7] makes plain, the authorities saw this as an instance of exemplary discipline – *pour encourager les autres* – demonstrating their own pre-eminence and letting students know the limits on their freedom of action. To do this they operated a disciplinary machinery which had previously, and then most rarely, been used for what may be termed "naughty boy" offences. The last occasion of its operation had been in 1951 when a student had tried to sell to a second-hand bookshop books from the library.[8]

In his book Kidd shows an implicit awareness that such a machinery would not be well suited to "political" offences, but he and his colleagues did not have the benefit of this hindsight at the time. As the whole tenor of his narrative reveals, the authorities had no conception whatsoever that what was really occurring was a fundamental shift in the legitimacy of their position.

In this particular instance the gap between the authorities' self-conception and the image held of them by the student body is indicated by the general feeling among students that a political struggle was in train between the School and its students. A university authority which is conceived in this way by its students has incurred a deep loss of legitimacy. We shall encounter this problem at several further stages of this chapter.

The boycott itself went fairly smoothly, and was quietly and efficiently controlled by students' union representatives. A diversionary activity was a demonstration by the Socialist Society and a fairly large circle of sympathisers. They sat outside the room where Adelstein's disciplinary proceedings were in progress, singing such protest songs as "We Shall Overcome", to the accompaniment of thoughtfully provided guitars. At the time the incident either amused or irritated people, several wondering how on earth the songs which had emerged from the struggle of the poverty-stricken American negro could be applied to a sedate and mannerly trial of solely formal significance, conducted under the auspices of English lawyers between members of the upper middle class and one of their junior generation.

But in retrospect and on closer examination this minor sit-in was not entirely out of context. It had struck me as I watched this group that they were in fact reliving the CND marches in which most of them had undoubtedly participated in past years. They all knew the songs, because they had sung them there. The guitars themselves had probably been carried from Aldermaston. Like everyone else, they were simply carrying on into the politics of their university lives the style and habits of politics to which they had become accustomed. There was a continuous potential tension between the socialists in their sit-in and the quiet boycott that

45

had been organised from the students' union. They seemed so entirely happy and at home in their little demonstration. When they contacted any of the rest of us and were forced to abide by our rules of protest, they became sullen and irritable. The activist politics of the new left had made its first real appearance at the LSE, but had failed to spread its atmosphere beyond the small confines of the singing protest.

Adelstein was not punished. We claimed a victory for direct action, the National Union of Students claimed a victory for its legal advice, and Harry Kidd has claimed that everything had gone according to plan from the point of view of the administration:

> "Before the meeting of the Standing Committee, Caine discussed the general situation informally over lunch with a group of governors and academic colleagues. There was general agreement that it was important to establish that an offence had been committed, and so to validate the Director's interpretation of the regulations, as well as to vindicate his authority in a difficult situation; on the other hand it was agreed that it would be right in the circumstances of this particular case not to seek the imposition of any penalty."[9]

Towards the end of term the School authorities extended their first invitation to the union to discuss student participation, and a group of us held two tiresome and futile meetings with members of the academic staff and the director. Apart from that the term ended quietly.

LENT TERM, 1967

As I have already stressed at several points, atmosphere is crucial to a radical student protest. For widespread success such a protest requires a deep change from normal relationships and modes of behaviour within the university. By December 1966 such an atmosphere was beginning to emerge at the LSE; by the end of the Christmas vacation, when everyone had been absent from the heady atmosphere of the

46

School for, of all contrasting atmospheres, their parental home at Christmastide, it had been entirely dissipated. Some of the more astute of the revolutionaries were, I suspect, aware of this, and knew that the only solution was to recreate the environment of protest.

The lead was taken by the late Marshall Bloom,* an American student who was chairman of the Graduate Students Association. Significantly, Bloom had much experience of the American civil rights movement, and had a distinguished record of organising sit-ins and the like on behalf of the American negroes in the south. He planned, under the auspices of the GSA, to hold a meeting at which the relevance of the experience of the US negroes and the students at Berkeley† could be applied to the campaign against the arrival of Walter Adams. As the date of the planned meeting approached (January 31) its theme became quite

* Marshall Bloom exemplified in his own life one of the patterns of progressive disillusion and alienation of a young American radical. A good student at university, he began doing research on race relations in the South when he was shortly out of his teens. He became deeply involved in the civil rights campaign, as a result of which he grew increasingly impatient with and deeply suspicious of constitutional political activity. At the same time he became much absorbed with the potentialities of direct action. In 1966 he came to the LSE as a graduate student, and as related above became deeply involved in the Adams issue when he sought to preach the doctrines of direct action to us. Although he became an official martyr of the student movement at the School, he was always somewhat alienated from the Marxists who dominated that movement; he resented what he regarded as their extreme dogmatism. Bloom belonged to the libertarian wing of the new left.

In summer 1967 he returned to the USA, where he played a prominent part in running a press agency for the American underground. Following a split between the dogmatists and the libertarians, he organised his own agency. But similar disputes continued, and Bloom finally took refuge from the constraints of both American society and new-left dogmatism by moving to a communal farm of hippies, where they raised animals and grew vegetables. Early in November 1969 he committed suicide by inhaling exhaust fumes from a motor car.

† During the Christmas vacation copies of a radical book[10] on the Berkeley troubles had been bought by many involved in the LSE movement.

47

clearly a discussion of ways of employing direct action to prevent Adams taking up his appointment. Posters advertising the meeting said that only students support-ing the idea should attend, and some posters libellously attributed to Adams a whole range of obscene and racialist remarks.

These posters were seen by the director, and regarding such discussion to be quite improper on premises that were under his auspices, he decided to ban the meeting. The ban was announced a couple of hours before the meeting was to take place and supporters of the meeting, who had been fearing that the Adams issue was so dead that few would attend it, now leapt into action with delight to publicise the ban. The meeting was to be held in a lecture room called the Old Theatre, where meetings of the union were always held. The area outside the hall was packed with about 600 students a quarter of an hour before the meeting was due to start. No doubt many were there from curiosity, but to judge from the mood of the meeting, the problem of the legitimacy of authority was rearing up again; students may not have been particularly interested in the meeting itself, but if the director was to ban it, then that was a challenge to a whole bundle of treasured rights. Why should he be allowed to do it?

Readers interested in the full proceedings of that extra-ordinary session outside the Old Theatre will find them accurately summarised by Harry Kidd,[11] who was, with the director, actively present. For our own purposes, the main point is that the director came down to argue the case, and by the end of the wrangling between him and the students, it was clear that we could hold the meeting in the students' union bar. The issue at stake was no longer a substantive one of whether a meeting could be held, but the formal principle of whether it should be held in the Old Theatre. It was in support of this principle that the students' mood deteriorated to one of uncontrolled anger, and they charged the doors of the theatre which were being guarded by porters. As is by now well known, Mr Edward Poole, a School porter who had a weak heart and had not been asked to help guard the doors, moved forward to help his colleagues. He collapsed and a gangway was made to carry him through the shouting and pushing mêlée of students. Although no direct physical assaults were being made on the porters, save pushing of the kind that is usually incurred by police guarding large crowds, Sir Sidney and Kidd were punched several times. Soon after the collapse of Poole, the students burst through the chain of porters and rushed into the theatre, which was in darkness, the director having ordered the fuses to be removed from the lighting system.

The scene inside the darkened theatre was extraordinary. Some students had lit candles, and small points of light illuminated agitated and gesticulating human forms as the theatre gradually filled. Several students were on the stage ready to start the scheduled meeting. Caine ascended the platform to announce that the porter had been hurt and to say that if the students would now leave the theatre there would be no victimisation. The theatre continued to fill, and was very noisy. Caine returned and made a vain attempt to still the noise. "The man has now died", he said, "Does that satisfy you?" There were enraged screams of "No!" from all sides of the theatre. Then the mood changed dramatically. It fell quiet, and students began slowly to leave.

Outside the Old Theatre someone was urging us to go back and continue with the meeting; others were attempting to have the meeting reorganised in the students' union bar. It was in that direction that many of us walked, dazed and worried. Several believed, or hoped, that Caine had lied about the porter's death in order to clear us from the theatre. In the bar Caine, to his lasting credit, was comforting weeping students, telling them they should not feel responsible. It was extraordinary how in the course of a few minutes people who had been regarding Caine with a bitter hatred could now find him a reassuring father figure. The School was closed for a day, and we all went home.

I have discussed these events in some detail because I consider they were extremely important in shaping the subsequent

49

attitude of a minority of us towards student protest. I had been in the midst of the crowd outside the Old Theatre, and although sympathetic to its opposition to Caine's ban, I had been unable to comprehend the depth of the anger that had been aroused on the abstract question of whether the Old Theatre should be charged or whether the meeting should be in the bar. I had been standing a few inches from Poole when he collapsed, and although I saw no one actually strike him, I concur entirely with Kidd's verdict:

". . . it remains my opinion that if it had been a normal day Poole would have had his tea and gone home."[12]

My immediate circle of friends was for a while completely overcome by a feeling of sickness and guilt at the thought that, for the sake of a small principle, we had been prepared to join in that rampaging crowd. In 1967 students at LSE who were involved in the events reacted principally to one of two incidents.* The majority reacted to the sit-in that was to follow in March, and emerged from that with an attitude of hostility to authority and an affection for direct action on the sit-in model. But for a minority of us this experience was overwhelmed by that of January 31, which we saw as an instance of temporary mob rule.

From then on my erstwhile enthusiasm for direct action and mass participation became coloured by the image of the enraged mob. Once such an attitude is formed on the basis of a powerful incident, one continues to find evidence for it, and in this case the role of the enraged mob in history is not a flattering story. If any single incident removed me from the company of the new mass-participatory left, it was January 31. Although subsequent events at the LSE have produced nothing quite similar, nothing has occurred since to refute my image of what is likely to happen when political action seeks as its predominant channel a mass impelled by hatred and passion.

The weeks following were extremely unpleasant. The

* I am indebted for this insight to my fellow student, Chris Brown.

right-wing of the student body saw a rare chance for revenge against the dominant left. A succession of anonymous pamphlets and leaflets appeared in the School, pointing fingers of blame in various directions. One, which was extremely long and so well produced that I continue to believe that no group of students had prepared it unaided, accused four students of fomenting the situation which was directly responsible for the death: Adelstein, Bloom, the editor of the college magazine and myself. In the union there were two extremely ugly meetings which almost toppled Adelstein and his council, but his political instincts recovered in time and he survived.

The School set up a committee of inquiry, to which many students went to give evidence so that the facts should be properly aired. We were assured that the committee's role was solely a fact-finding one, and several of us gave evidence on that basis alone. Subsequently the evidence was given to the School authorities, who used it as the basis of the case for the prosecution in disciplinary proceedings; members of the law department acting as defence counsel were not permitted to make use of it. As someone who had given evidence to the committee, I regarded this as a cynical betrayal of trust by the School which, despite my misgivings about the development of protest, greatly increased my readiness to join the onslaught on them a few weeks later.

So for a second time the School's disciplinary machinery was brought into operation against the student protest movement, this time against Adelstein, Bloom and four members of the students' union council, on the grounds that they had been responsible for allowing the meeting of January 31 to proceed after it had been banned. Again, I shall refer those who seek more factual detail of the trial to Harry Kidd's account;[13] our main concern in this narrative is to trace the growth of a student movement, how it took shape, and the sources from which it fed.

As the arrangements for the trial were being made, the dispute between the militants and the moderates among activist students became sharper and more acrimonious. The

51

basis of the dispute was becoming clearer; it existed between those who sought to use legal, bureaucratic channels as much as possible, using direct action purely as an instrumental political lever of last resort, and those who sought to create a protest movement rooted in the use of direct action as the only valid means of political procedure. In both cases the view was related to the familiar division in left-wing politics between reformists and revolutionaries, and in nearly all instances wider political affiliations were related to the stance adopted on this particular issue. The Socialist Society wanted us to organise demonstrations and protests throughout the trial, and sought to require the students concerned not to appear before the tribunal. Those of us on the reformist wing characteristically preferred to concentrate on ensuring that the trial was "fair", and that the members of the tribunal were not enraged by untoward protests about their activities. We also considered it immoral to dictate to the students about to be tried what their own behaviour should be. Within the union the two sides were evenly matched, but we succeeded in maintaining the moderate line throughout the trial, which six students (including myself) were able to attend as observers.

The trial dragged on for some weeks. Eventually it closed and the tribunal prepared its verdict. A union meeting had been scheduled for the time of announcement of the result. The four members of council were found not guilty, but Adelstein and Bloom were suspended for the rest of the year. The reformist policy within the student body had failed entirely. There was nothing left but to support the policy of the militants, which was to "sit-in" immediately. The motion to support an occupation was in fact proposed by the new president of the Students Union, Peter Watherston, chairman of the Conservative Society. Whatever Watherston had understood by "sit-in", he had not envisaged what was to take place among the student body for the following nine days. The Socialist Society had, and they had started the occupation before the meeting had concluded its business.

The scene outside the Old Theatre, with students sitting

down and packing the main entrance hall to the School, was very similar to that which had been present outside the disciplinary hearing in December; only this time instead of being a small group on the fringe of the protest, the Socialist Society was setting the tone for the whole activity. During that week the revolutionaries achieved their objective for the first time at LSE; they created the prevailing atmosphere within which we all had to move. We stayed in the college Monday night, and for the whole of the week between 200 and 800 people were spending their nights in the barricaded building. As the week progressed, our ranks were supplemented by an anonymous crowd of young people, some from other universities, others from nowhere in particular, who joined the protest. During the day many students continued to use the library, and classes and lectures still continued. But the most obvious fact about LSE at that time was that a large group of students filled the major entrance hall or carried on a variety of supplementary activities associated with the protest throughout the day and prevented it being closed at night.

As before, I am not concerned to relate detailed events, but to point out the characteristics of the movement and the forms of solidarity that there developed. With the collapse of the moderate approach, the whole edifice of established student politics, such as it was, collapsed. The forms of union debate were continued; indeed, the union was in virtually continuous session. But the constraints of the constitution and proper procedure appeared gauche, inappropriate, almost embarrassing. A new mode of discussion, a new range of emotions and responses was being explored. Far more appropriate than the forms of union debate were the *extempore* exhortatory meetings that would spring up, sometimes among the crowd outside the Old Theatre, sometimes within it. A series of speakers would harangue the audience; the more extreme their stance, the more sympathetic the audience. Words like "struggle", "the situation within which we find ourselves", "solidarity", "principles" would win applause. Such expressions as "we must act with

53

caution", "careful", "the most appropriate means of achieving our ends" would earn a difficult, perhaps impossible, hearing.

There were few elected leaders, but there were some individuals who, when they spoke, would be received in awe; to interrupt or heckle them would be to invite a ferocious response from the crowd. Meetings would go on long into the night in the Old Theatre, usually presided over by Richard Kuper, a brilliant orator, who would sit on the platform cross-legged, smoking a pipe.

These events went on for several days. The sense of intensity was greatly increased by the surprising prominence accorded to us by the Press, television and radio. If the comment was often hostile and distorted, this only led to a feeling of solidarity. Several non-students addressed us during the week. Members of staff taking a "liberal compromise" viewpoint were unwelcome, as were the occasional Labour MPs, who represented a rude intrusion of the political world against which the protest was becoming directed as much as against the School authorities. A shop steward who brought a resolution of support from his branch late one night was received ecstatically. Sometimes the meetings would take on the characteristics of an early revivalist meeting, as individuals would tell us how they had come to experience a new view of life in the course of the sit-in. Some were incited to acts of individual "heroism", such as the group which embarked on a bizarre invasion of the administration building early one morning, or the individuals who undertook a hunger strike.

The arguments which had led myself, and, I suspect, many of my friends, to participate in the sit-in had been couched very much in orthodox political terms: we had been the victims of an arbitrary authority, and it was therefore necessary, in order to enforce on the authorities a new commitment to reasonable procedures, to assert some countervailing power of our own. Alternatively, by embarrassing the authorities publicly, we could force them to back down. If that failed, we may hope to create such chaos that the Department

54

of Education and Science would be forced to intervene, a development which some of us naïvely believed would be entirely to the students' advantage. Thus I had viewed the sit-in as a purely instrumental activity: an unpleasant, not to say intensely uncomfortable, means to a desired end. As the week progressed it became clear how far out of touch such a view had been, although it is only in retrospect that I appreciate the nature of the divergence between the revolutionaries and the "moderates".

For the emergent leaders who set the tone of LSE over the whole of that period, the sit-in was partly an end in itself. It was a form of mass participative activity which had broken down the existing structures of behaviour and created its own forms of experience. It was seen partly as an educative experience, an education involving the "whole man", and not simply the intellectualised aspects of man to which conventional education made its approach. Emotional tension was of course high. We had embarked on a novel, potentially dangerous course of action; we were tired; we were aware of the almost unanimous hostility of the outside world, which penetrated our stronghold through the editorial columns of the newspapers and through the occasional nocturnal visits to the School of inebriated members of the bourgeoisie.

The atmosphere of unreality was heightened by the growth among our number of a group of hippies,* who spent much of the time "high" on pot. A further illusion of self sufficiency was the operation of a canteen that served late snacks and breakfasts. In this way the sit-in became not so much a part of the sojourn in the wilderness for the chosen people of the revolution, but a trailer for the Promised Land itself. This experience, on an incredibly small and acknowledgedly unrealistic scale, was what the revolutionaries had spoken of when they dreamed of a new kind of politics, a new freedom from the constraints of mundane authority, a new immediacy of personal relations, a breaking down of the requirements of the roles we were forced to occupy in everyday life. On the

* It will be recalled that summer 1967 was the season of the "flower children".

55

occasions when Sir Sidney would come to speak to us in the Old Theatre during that week, he would be asked to do certain things to secure the liberation of Adelstein and Bloom. He would reply that he was in no position to do this as director of the School; he had no power to act, and so forth. The hostility that this would arouse was only partly the hostility of people frustrated by failure to achieve their objectives. It was also the hostility engendered by confrontation between the "bureaucrat" and the existentialist; the clash between the occupier of a formal role whose constraints he acknowledges, and the libertarian who is absolute in his rejection of role obligations and situational constraints.*

People spoke of the "community" that had been created during the sit-in; they valued the "concrete" nature of the immediacy of experience. They placed great stress on "spontaneity" and on the positive value of mass participative action. It was wrong to talk about tactics, to try to plan what our next moves should be, for that imposed a blueprint, lacked spontaneity and smacked of the calculating world outside; it also meant allowing exogenous factors to impinge on our total autonomy, our total ability to control our lives. It was more than wrong to do such things; it was treacherous. One was either committed or one had sold out. Once a course had been set by the mass,† one had to abide by it. How else can matters be decided in a mass situation that has rejected calculation? For a week we lived in a world of the eternal present, the heritage of the immediate past being destroyed and the future being left to develop according to the dictates of constant spontaneity.

I do not mean by all this that the leaders of the left lost sight of the immediate objectives of the sit-in. Of these they were ever conscious. But the actual *process* of protest was

---

* The group of student militants which has most profoundly rejected all obligations of role are the Situationists (see Chapter Four, p. 104).

† Although one may speak of a course "set by the mass", the fact that severe restrictions were placed on the kind of discussion that was permissible imposed limitations on the ability of decisions to be "democratic" in any usually accepted meaning of that term.

raised to a position of value in its own right alongside these objectives, and became an issue of its own. It is here desirable to point out a difference in emphasis on these matters between the old-guard Marxists, who were mainly interested in developing their model of direct action, and the anarchists, libertarians and Americans, who were interested in building a community. The differences among these different factions were not particularly important at this time; two years later they were to assume far greater significance.

A group of those involved in these events subsequently made a film of the sit-in. Towards the end of this film there is a long and desultory discussion among some students which concentrates almost entirely on this point about the experience of community. About twelve months after the sit-in I attended a dinner given at the School for the previous year's graduates. One of them, a girl, made one of the evening's speeches; her main point was to say that the only "real" and "valid" experience she had had at LSE had been the sit-in. I consider this question to be of great importance to an understanding of student protest, and shall return to it at a more analytical level in later chapters (Chapters Six and Eight). This yearning for involvement, for community, for immediacy and concreteness has also figured in the rhetoric of protest elsewhere in Britain and in France, Germany and the USA.

By the end of the week the sitters-in were becoming increasingly divided. Those on the moderate wing felt that they had done all they could, that the sit-in would soon begin to break down with the onset of the Easter vacation the coming Tuesday, and that nothing further could be done for Adelstein and Bloom. It was the classic pessimistic acceptance of the inevitable that is so often typical of saddened liberals. It distinguishes them from thorough-going reactionaries and revolutionaries alike, to the liberals' discredit.* The revolutionaries, on the other hand, could not bear the thought of

---

* An attack on what he calls the "possibilists" forms a major theme of Hal Draper's[14] study of Berkeley. By it he means those among the dissenting staff and students who would assess a situation in terms of the usual possibilities of the political game, and decide on that basis whether

ending the sit-in. The idea that we should be prepared to end what one of them had described as the most beautiful experience of his life for the purely tactical reason that the thing was likely to fold up at the end of term angered them as much as did their belief that we were prepared to "sacrifice" Adelstein and Bloom. (By now the element of "sacrifice" had become somewhat symbolic, as the suspensions on the two had been attenuated in concessions made by the authorities during the week. These concessions together with the fact that sympathetic members of staff would probably have ensured that the two had at least equal tuition as other students, meant that there was far more danger of "sacrificing" the careers of some hundreds of students if the sit-in continued into the summer examination term.)

On the Friday night a long and acrimonious debate was started, at about 10.00 pm, in the course of which all these issues were raised and churned over. The occasion of the debate was the Standing Committee's announcement of concessions. Well over 800 people were in attendance. We adjourned at 2.00 am, and reconvened at 1.00 pm on the Saturday. The debate ended at about 7.00 pm. The moderates won; the protest would be lifted the coming Tuesday.

The revolutionaries, tired, embittered and disillusioned, took their defeat badly. During the weekend they continued to display their rejection of the union's decision, and Watherston wisely agreed to hold a further meeting on the Monday at which a superbly balanced compromise motion was discussed and accepted. This called for the suspension of the sit-in on Tuesday, but also stated that throughout the

---

a course of action was worth pursuing. This is contrasted with the course of the militants, who would act according to principles without fine means-end calculations, and would therefore often be able to force a solution through the alleged constraints of the situation. A similar idea is contained in Cohn-Bendit's concept of revolutionary *élan*. The whole idea is closely related to the revolutionary's frustration with the constraints of constitutional politics in modern society, to which we have already referred on several occasions.

vacation the protest would be continued in the form of a "free university", while the sit-in itself would be restarted on the first day of the summer term if the suspensions on Adelstein and Bloom had not been lifted.

Thus in substance the moderates kept their victory, while the form of the motion appeared to satisfy the militants' desire for a fight to the bitter end. Some of the more astute militants still felt betrayed; they guessed (accurately) that the moderates had calculated that by the start of the new term the whole thing would have dissipated. The militants gave themselves solace in the formula "The shop stewards can't strike if the workers don't want to", and the Marxists among them went off to the Barbican building site where they gave considerable assistance to the pickets in a particularly long and bitter strike at a site of Mytons Ltd. Some of them probably felt that this was a more satisfactory activity than a sit-in by students who were, after all, members of the bourgeoisie. Although the far left had successfully controlled the articulation of the LSE protest, they had not really been able to place the struggle against the School authorities in the wider context of a struggle against capitalism which most of them quite genuinely believed it was. This was remedied in the pamphlet[15] subsequently published on the events by the Socialist Society, which included an analysis of how the LSE governors were an important segment of the British ruling class. Significantly, the back cover of the pamphlet showed a picture of the builders of the Barbican in a confrontation with the Metropolitan Police. The heading was "Myton Men in Direct Action".

The free university that was in some curious way to maintain the protest during the vacation absorbed the energy of that element of the left less Marxist and proletarian in its orientation. This group was overwhelmingly American in membership. The relationship between a free university and the protest was rather abstract and therefore doomed to a half-hearted existence and an early demise.

But whatever its weaknesses in practice, the theory of the free university was elegantly complete. The sit-in had been a protest against a particular decision of the School authorities, but that decision had been just one instance of a regime that was restrictive and instrumental in the interests of the ruling class. The education provided at LSE was similarly an expression of this regime. Therefore an effective protest could be mounted in the form of a free university that challenged this regime at all points in its own existence. Thus enormous importance was placed by the organisers of the venture on the need to be able to continue sessions into the night after the time that the school was normally closed; even time had become an instrument of the ruling class, it would seem. The dictates of authority had to be countermanded at every turn. The seminars that made up the free university would, of course, be extremely open, with a minimum of structure. Invited outside speakers often had to accept when they arrived that they and their prepared address were given no greater status than any *ad hoc* comment by a member of the audience. As may be expected, this refusal to accept any constraints of formal structure led to a deadening uniformity as people peddled their hobby-horses at every possible opportunity.

Meanwhile, in the formal structured channels of the School's machinery, progress was being made on the issue of the suspensions. Towards the end of the sit-in a whole variety of channels of communication had been opened up between staff and students. I had shared in several of these, and found them among the most rewarding exercises of the whole episode. However disagreeable the sit-in was, it changed the level of staff-student discourse at the LSE and made it necessary for at least a proportion of members of staff to treat students with a new level of respect that has in some ways continued from that time on. The main fruit of these initial discussions was the establishment of the "ten-ten committee", a peculiarly named body comprising ten members of the academic staff and ten students.

In a rare moment of old-fashioned political prescience the students' union had balanced the student membership of this committee with five militants and five "moderates". The

60

latter group included Watherston and myself, although the other three were not so distant from the militant position. Our first objective on the committee was to encourage it to seek a re-opening of the Adelstein-Bloom issue with the Court of Governors. This was accomplished. Watherston appeared before the Court and subsequently performed with success the near-impossible task of negotiating an agreed solution between that group of somewhat disgruntled and dignified gentlemen and the two student *prime donne*.

On the wider issues that the committee was to discuss, those of student participation, there was far less progress. Some of the academics were tiresome in a way that only a committee of university teachers can be, while the revolutionary students had no intention of doing otherwise than proposing impossible schemes for the government of the college. It was part of the problem of a thorough-going anti-reformist revolutionary. They found it acceptable to work for immediate negative causes like the Adelstein-Bloom suspension, mainly with the objective of building within the protest an on-going revolutionary movement; but it was quite impossible for them to work for positive structural reforms. This was partly because they do not believe any reform can be achieved in such a structure as the LSE without an international socialist revolution, and partly because a movement that gains its strength and vitality from its ability to take up strong and uncompromising stands would lose its very *raison d'être* if it had any truck with the proceedings of liberal compromise. Once the Adelstein-Bloom issue had been dispatched within the committee, the revolutionaries' only objective was to ensure that the committee would soon disintegrate. An innocuous statement from the academic members proved the *casus belli*, we walked out and the committee disbanded. A second committee which had been set up to reform the disciplinary regulations met a very similar fate.

SUMMER TERM, 1967

All this had happened during the Easter vacation. The following summer term saw a considerable change. The effect of the return to parental homes had had its expected effect on the atmosphere of the student body except among the hippy group, who had in any case probably stayed together during the holidays. They set the tone of union meetings; playing flutes, squirting water pistols and gradually draining of any vestigial reality the idea of the LSE students' union being a serious force within the school.

The leaders of the revolutionaries were still together too, but with the lifting of the suspensions they lacked a cause and a movement. Their main activity of the term was to join with a group of persons not concerned with LSE in an invasion of the Greek Embassy some time after the colonels' *coup d'état*, from whence they broadcast messages of liberation on a short-wave radio to Athens. For this they earned a few nights in jail, a good deal of admiration and respect and a large donation from students' union funds towards their legal costs. The only other development of note that summer was the election of five students to the committee on the machinery of government of the School, whose membership comprised about nine each of governors and academic staff. The militants boycotted the committee for the same reasons that they had ended the "ten-ten committee", but the union backed it. The five students were Adelstein, Watherston, Chris Middleton (secretary of the students' union), Richard Atkinson, a graduate student of the left whose precise political position among the student factions was difficult to determine,* and myself. As yet another exercise in staff-student discussions of student participation lumbered into progress, the academic year ended.

CONCLUSION

At this point we may usefully summarise the major developments in the student movement since those early rumblings

---

* Atkinson had incurred the wrath of the Socialist Society by declaring in, of all places, the *Daily Telegraph* weekend supplement: "The working class has ceased to exist."[16]

in 1965. In a very short time a protest movement of distinctive tone and style had flared into life, held sway over the college for eight days, and gone into decline. Brief though its full period of existence was, it bore sufficiently close relationship to the kind of movement that had been generated at Berkeley, and later at other universities in the USA, France and Germany, to justify consideration. As has been hinted at here, and as is discussed more fully at other points in this book, the essence of this movement was its expression of a kind of politics shaped in direct and conscious opposition to the politics of the conventional world. The fact that the importance of the protest itself to that political world was negligible does not affect its self-conception. Throughout all the debates between revolutionaries and constitutionalists, militants and moderates, an underlying consciousness on both sides of the wider political implications of the positions being adopted was ever present, and would frequently be made quite explicit.

As to the issues of the protests, there had from the outset been a concern with wider politics. The Adams issue only came alight because of the Rhodesian connection. The hostility incurred by the protest from the press and from Conservative and Liberal politicians during the actual sit-in strengthened these feelings, and the role of the Court of Governors was consistent with the theory of the Socialist Society that the challenge we had posed to the "system" was more than symbolic.

The issue of participation had also existed from the outset, although it had frequently been submerged. As soon as an immediate conflict had been quietened, the response of both staff and students was to start discussions on student participation. Closely related was the question of discipline and the changing student attitudes to the rights of the School authorities to discipline for "political" offences, which had now been raised in practical and immediate terms on two occasions.

In sum, the position of students within a university community was changing in ways that, although then not clearly understood, have now become commonplace. Meanwhile, this whole change was taking place against a wider context of the political methods and political styles which were undergoing considerable scrutiny by young people on the political left in a period of Labour Government. The university and its issues seemed to be a part of the wider canvas of a world dominated by a sinister and irresponsible power, and provided scope for a testing of new approaches and new methods. Although the importance of the conflict between staff and students obscured it at the time, the university was not only the adversary, but also a battle-ground, perhaps a recruiting ground, for the militant students. This was to become much clearer twelve months and more later.

REFERENCES

1. The Socialist Society, LSE, *LSE's New Director: A Report on Walter Adams*, 1966
2. Crick, B., *In Defence of Politics*, 1962, pp 134–5
3. *The Times*, October 25 1966
4. Kidd, H., *The Trouble at LSE 1966–7*, 1969, pp 9, 10
5. *ibid*, pp 29–35
6. *The Times*, October 29 1966
7. Kidd, *op cit*, p 29 et seq
8. *ibid*, p 10
9. *ibid*, p 29
10. Draper, H., *Berkeley: The New Student Revolt*, 1966
11. Kidd, *op cit*, ch 4
12. *ibid*, p 53
13. *ibid*, ch 6
14. Draper, *op cit*
15. The Socialist Society, LSE, *LSE: What It Is and How We Fought It*, 1967
16. *Daily Telegraph* weekend supplement, June 28, 1968

CHAPTER THREE

Student Revolt at LSE, 1967–69

The old politics reasserted its ascendancy over the new at the start of the academic year 1967–8 at the LSE. Walter Adams took his place as director with scarcely a murmur from the student body. Watherston succeeded in keeping a shaky peace among the factions of the students' union, and most students who were at all interested were satisfied to wait for the report of the machinery of government committee before reassessing their attitude to the School and its authorities.

Within that committee halting progress was being made as the Michaelmas term wore on. Student representation could now be seriously discussed with only a couple of the lay governors expressing a sense of outrage. But within the ranks of the five student members divisions were growing. Watherston and myself had begun to concentrate on getting as good a result as possible from the committee, while the radical instincts of Atkinson and Middleton were becoming restless. Adelstein, who was in Cuba for most of the time, returned to join Atkinson and Middleton. Their objective was not only a far higher degree of student representation, but also a vastly reduced role for the lay governors. Allied with this, they wanted the committee to broaden its horizons to examine the role of university education within the late-capitalist economy and its demands of the education system.

By the time the committee reported,[1] with a flurry of notes of dissent, Middleton had resigned and Atkinson and Adelstein signed a minority report prepared by the former.[2] It was a longer document than the majority report, and is in itself a substantial example of the thinking of the student left, being a few shades to the right of the hard-line Marxists.

It expressed considerable dissatisfaction with the dominance of lay governors in the School, and sought a wider range of social background among these governors, to whom it assigned a much diminished role in the School's government. The major structure of the college's government would be reorganised to allow virtual parity between staff and students in decision-making. But the report was not satisfied with a reform limited to the LSE's internal arrangements. It was concerned at the direction of higher educational policy under the Labour Government, and saw this as a major threat against which staff and students had a united interest:

"It should be pretty clear that in encouraging the Binary System the Labour Government, Civil Service, and the pressures on them, wanted to create, through the 'public sector', a large, state-tied, and industrially oriented training ground for students. Then it intends slowly to remove and alter the independence and general education orientation of the Universities until they become indistinguishable from the élite of the technical colleges. Only then would Higher Education be fulfilling the needs held out to it by the 'technological revolution' of Mr Wilson's vision."[3]

In its approach to education as such, the minority report sought to wear down the idea of an academic hierarchy and staff-student divisions by stressing the creative aspects of education and resisting attempts at "packaging" and "grading" students. The point was related to the former one of state and industrial interference. Creativity and freedom were seen as opposed to the demands being made by industry and state, while the grading and direction involved in concepts of academic hierarchy were seen as related to the need by employers for specialised and highly disciplined recruits. Therefore the resolution of internal demands by students for participation was seen as inextricably linked to wider political problems of power.[4]

Watherston and I, in our note of dissent from the report,[5]

concentrated on urging a greater degree of student representation on certain committees. The report was due to appear
in March. By February the mood within the students' union
was becoming lively again. Atkinson had created a stir by
publishing an acrimonious statement about the proceedings
of the committee and claiming that it had tried to censor him.
Interest was also aroused by the fact that elections for the
presidency of the students' union were again due, and Middleton and I were candidates. When the union came to debate the report the Socialist Society, frustrated at the failure
of the movement they had created, determined that the old
form of union politics should not be allowed to progress
either. They made use of persistent noise and clamour to
hinder discussion. The union was split three ways. The
Socialist Society, fearing the possibility that the union would
completely accept the politics of liberal compromise, produced their own proposals for government of the college by
a general assembly of all staff, students, porters, administration, kitchen staff and cleaners. I have yet to convince myself
that the highly intelligent individuals who put this idea forward really believed in it, despite their insistent avowals of
sincerity. (The plan does, of course, faithfully represent some
of the main tenets of faith of the new left, and these are discussed in Chapter Five.)

Atkinson, Adelstein and Middleton put forward the minority report, and Watherston and I defended the majority
report, as amended by our note of dissent. It was probably
inherent in the structure of such a three-sided debate that the
"middle course", that of Atkinson, should triumph. The
union defeated both the Socialist Society's proposals and
those of Watherston and myself, and voted for the minority
report, although a few days previously I had been elected
president of the union with Middleton coming third out of
five candidates. Not long afterwards the academic board, for
entirely separate reasons, also rejected the report of the
machinery of government committee, and the whole question
of student representation was once again put back out of immediate discussion within LSE. The second term of 1967–8

ended shortly afterwards. This had been LSE's "quiet year". It is difficult to know how much to attribute to the actions of individuals in a situation that seems so much to be governed by wider social currents, as the LSE certainly was. But I suspect that a fair proportion of the disaster that beset us over the ensuing twelve months was partly my fault. The trouble in this respect lay with my whole approach. I had, as related in the previous chapter, been an early supporter of experimentation with notions of direct action, but in my scheme it had been set within the wider context of an orthodox pluralist political system. Direct action was useful as a means of putting pressure on a system that would rigidify in the absence of such pressure. This was a far cry from the notions being developed by the revolutionary left, and I still entertained hopes of being able to swing the direction of student protest into a different mode. I thus paradoxically had a more direct enmity towards the militants than a Conservative like Watherston, who was content to manage and balance the different forces within the union with the sole objective of ensuring stability and peace.

I had also worked out that the left's strength lay partly in their ability to articulate a dramatic position, to seize the initiative in action, and to attract attention within both the college and the outside media. It was all part of the revolutionary *élan*. Through the excitement of deep emotions, principally the emotion of hatred, they could manipulate the passions that were essential to their brand of politics. In this exercise I had no wish to compete, but I did seek to go part of the way by stealing the initiative in action, and by giving character to the reformist movement among the student body, such as it was, through a declared position of opposition to the left on the one hand and determined pursuit of the objectives of participation, and so forth, on the other. But a policy of deliberately raising the temperature of affairs was, given the circumstances, bound to play into the hands of the revolutionaries, for only they were prepared to exploit the situation created by such a heightened tension. Heightened

68

tension has to be governed in its expression by certain constraints, or it becomes chaos. If the procedures of the School were respected and/or feared by the student body, then these would have channelled political expression.

But this was not the case. Through the slowness in implementing reforms in the direction of participation the authorities had lost the loyalty of many students. Further the School's stand on the two disciplinary cases had been such as to capture the worst of two worlds. First, by taking disciplinary action on poorly defensible grounds, they had sacrificed respect. Second, on then succumbing to pressure, they had lost the credibility that adheres to a firm, hard stand. Only a very narrow line stood between the normal life of the School and widespread disaffection by much of the student body. In not too long a time that line was to be crossed.

In the meantime a strategy of student politics based on implicit acceptance of the School's procedures was extremely vulnerable; such was my position. The far left, on the other hand, had an alternative set of constraints in which heightened political tempers could be channelled. In practice a very narrow and dogmatic channel, it had an illusion of liberation by the contrast it displayed to the bureaucratic, orthodox-political modes of operation of the School and the students' union. The result of my policy was therefore to create a head of steam that could work only to the advantage of my opponents.

SUMMER TERM, 1968

But initially matters started well enough. During the Easter vacation Enoch Powell made the first of his racialist speeches. Term was to start a few days later, and the Conservative Society had invited Powell to speak at the School shortly afterwards. The policy that had been emerging at several universities in the case of impending visits by unpopular speakers was to disrupt the meeting and render it impossible through, of course, mass activity and mass disruption. Both interfering directly with freedom of speech and using a mob to do so were offensive to my political instincts, and I suspected that this would be planned by the Socialist Society. There was a need for a more appropriate response. The extent of the publicity being given to Powell was surely the result of a certain created mood in politics; therefore the proper attack was to set going a counter mood that would encourage the deprecation of Powellite stands. It seemed that we had at LSE a chance to play a tiny part in helping to create that mood, so I decided to write an open letter to Powell informing him why, since LSE was a multi-racial college and an academic institution, it was highly undesirable that he should appear on our premises at such a time. The letter achieved in fact far more publicity than I had anticipated, and Powell did not come to the LSE, though this was more the result of panic at the thought of impending chaos on the part of the Conservative Society leadership than because of my letter. The Socialist Society was furious at what I had done, and declared that to oppose Powell in the way I had adopted was "racialist". To such depths runs the conflict between the new left and an older radicalism.

The only other events of note that term were two sit-ins by the Socialist Society – half-hearted one-night stands that represented a vain attempt to recapture the atmosphere of March 1967. The issues of the sit-ins were, in the first case, solidarity with the French students, who were in the midst of their immense conflict with the Fifth Republic, and in the second, the occasion of the inaugural conference at the School of the Revolutionary Socialist Students Federation. These incidents, minor in scope, made one point very plain. Student revolt did not need actions by the authorities to justify the occupation of a university building; the academic institution was just a convenient location for the development of the communal movement of the kind that had lived for nine days in March 1967. This introduced a dangerous new element of instability in the situation; if the left could find an external issue capable of attracting wide support, the situation would be completely beyond the control of reforming gestures by the university. The only safety rested in the difficulty of achieving this widespread support on an external matter.

On both these occasions I took steps to point out the irrelevance of the demonstrations to LSE's problems. By the end of the term I think it had become clear to the left that I was no longer the diffident sympathiser I had previously been, but I was becoming an outright opponent. I had also broken an important tacit agreement. It had been the fashion during Watherston's presidency for the "moderates" to allow the left to make all the running in terms of action, initiative and publicity; in exchange for this passivity, Watherston had been permitted by the left to stay in office. By the various public attacks I had made on the left by the end of the summer term it was obvious that I had not acknowledged my side of such an understanding. I should have hardly been surprised that they then determined not to honour theirs.

MICHAELMAS TERM, 1968

When the new academic year opened the following October, the issue of representation appeared again. The Academic Board were producing proposals based on the majority report of the machinery of government committee, and I was invited, with the union council, to take part in the discussions. There was much dissatisfaction in the union that we were doing so when the union's declared policy was acceptance of the minority report. But it seemed to me that union policy could always be changed with proper organisation of the vote. Besides, my experience of the students' union's democracy in operation had not been such as to invoke my deep respect.

A policy was emerging from the Academic Board that showed a degree of willingness to exceed their previous proposals. They still acted with a painful caution and an amusing wariness. The decision to allow the union council to attend discussions followed a lengthy debate and was treated as a matter of great moment. One felt as though one were Pandora's box. We were carefully removed from the room before votes were taken. Nevertheless, the Board was moving in our direction.

I considered that the gap between the Board's position and that which would best serve students' interests was a negotiable distance. But for meaningful negotiations to be possible, the union would have to cease its current posture. The Board would have no incentive to negotiate with the union unless it could be convinced that progress was possible.

I therefore called a special meeting of the union on October 17 to consider the new position of the Academic Board and the response to it that the union council considered appropriate. On the morning of the meeting we learned that an urgency resolution would be brought to it, calling for the occupation of the School on the weekend of October 25–27 to hold it as a place of sanctuary, medical assistance and political discussion for all-comers to the vast demonstration against the war in Vietnam planned for that weekend in London, which by all available information was likely to be a bloody affair.*

The idea seemed so extraordinary that I did not take it seriously. Why take over the LSE to protest against the American Government? I had not yet fully appreciated that the School was simply a battle-ground and recruiting area for protest, and that the authorities did not have to be the direct target of attack. In any case, in the fully fledged theory of the far left there is no such thing as individual "authorities"; there is just one continuous, monolithic "authority":

"The path from the examination-room to the paddy-fields of Vietnam may appear to be a rather long and devious trek; this is because of our neat habit of separating issues into their 'well-defined' compartments – defined of course by academics who function in the main, as the intellectual servants of the 'status quo'. . . . But the path of

* The eventual passivity of the demonstration was used by the left at LSE and elsewhere as evidence that the Establishment had panicked at its own scare-mongering. The call for "a place of sanctuary and medical assistance" hardly justifies the view that fears of the events of that weekend were limited to non-supporters of the demonstration.

Student Power rejects this segmentation of our thought-processes, this narrow channelling of the mind. . . . There is a social pattern to these events which can be traced back to the social and economic organisation of societies – in other words examinations and support for the American policy in Vietnam – both emanate from a certain type of society, from the same social set-up known as monopoly capitalism in Britain today."[6]

In addition to being bizarre, the motion could certainly not be debated at an emergency meeting called to discuss an entirely different issue. Of course, it was so discussed, and more amazingly it was passed, by a meeting obviously biased in composition as a result of the lack of publicity the motion had received. The motion on representation that I had brought to the meeting, mainly as the result of left-wing insistence that I stop negotiating with the Academic Board without consulting the union, lay undiscussed; they had bigger fish to fry now.

A large group of students, mainly connected with the Conservative Society, were outraged at what had been done. They demanded a new meeting to rediscuss the question. I told them that this would only be possible if they could present the union council with sufficient evidence that there was widespread discontent with the results of the vote. This they proceeded to do in the form of a petition signed by almost a thousand students. The Socialist Society were furious, and there were ugly scenes when they confronted petitioners. Some of them developed an extraordinary theory of how the petition was a reactionary device, as it provided for an alienated form of participation that was not a "real" experience.

The second meeting was called, and was attended by about 1,200 students. This was the largest attendance at a union meeting at the LSE up to that time. The meeting lasted from 10.30 am to 2.30 pm. The debate was long and sometimes bitter. I gave as my opposition to the projected occupation the argument that this was a misuse of university buildings; behind the occupation was the theory that the university as an institution should be committed to a particular side in a

73

dispute. This seemed to me to threaten the freedoms of the university in the same way as would have occurred had the School offered sanctuary during the weekend to the Metropolitan Police controlling the demonstration. Further, I disapproved of the use of the sit-in weapon when we were not in dispute with the School authorities. It was not the function of a university to act as a battle-ground. Supporters of the occupation used several arguments, among them being the familiar one that the jealously guarded rights and freedoms of the university were irrelevant compared with the horrors of Vietnam. It was also argued that academic autonomy was in any case a myth, since the university was but the instrument of the ruling class; which ruling class was also the oppressor in Vietnam.

In other words, the issues in this debate were central to the whole framework of the new left's concept of both the university and the political system. For the new left such activities as the Vietnam occupation were not only acceptable uses of a university, but about the only uses worth accepting. It would, of course, also provide a further opportunity for recapturing that treasured atmosphere of March 1967.

When it came to the vote, the opposition to the occupation had a majority of 60. In my view a majority of 60 in an electorate of 1,200 is, though close, clear and convincing. By no rule of fairness could a recount be considered necessary, especially as people began streaming from the hall as soon as the vote was completed. It was not the supporters of the occupation who were leaving the hall; they were bellowing for a recount. The chairman of the meeting, a member of the academic staff, Dr Meghnad Desai, acceded to their demand. His decision must have been the result of the confusion and the insistent screaming of the supporters of occupation. As expected, in the recount our majority was reduced to six. The revolutionaries were elated; pandemonium broke out. I heard a group of the occupation supporters telling each other to press for a second recount, as our supporters were continuing to leave. They would then obviously have a majority. I had no option but to announce to the meeting that we should consider the union to be neutral; opponents of the occupation would not be able to claim that it would be in defiance of the union's policy, which would have laid occupiers open to easily justified discipline by the School. Nor would the demonstrators be able to claim they were acting as agents of the union, able to plead union support should difficulties arise. It was a shabby result. I was convinced we had been cheated.

Meanwhile the School authorities had been fearful of possible damage to the School property, including the priceless library, in the event of this occupation by a group of unknown size and identity. Only the weekend beforehand someone associated with the Vietnam protest movement had set off a bomb in the Imperial War Museum. Adams issued a statement in the name of the Court of Governors stating that he had authority to close the School in the event of the occupation taking place. The effect of this on the student body and a good number of the staff was extraordinary. People who previously had opposed the occupation now supported it for no other reason than that the Governors had intervened. It is difficult to conceive of a worse position for an authority than that wherein its actions against a particular group turn that group's former opponents into its allies. This was the position now reached by the LSE authorities. The fragile hold of their position (having lost both the respect of consent and that of fear), their dilatoriness on student representation, and the widespread resentment of this interference by a group of laymen whose connections with the School often seemed tenuous, had made their mark. If the statement had been issued in the name of the academic board there was a slight possibility that the responses would have been different. While making this point it should, however, be pointed out that the difference would have been almost entirely one of appearance.

The Standing Committee of the Court of Governors includes members of the academic staff in addition to lay governors, and in practice the latter have usually been prepared to adhere closely to the advice of the former. Most of

75

the detailed proposals of the School for firm action have come from the academic rather than the lay members of the court; it could well be argued that having such statements made in the name of the governors has the effect of minimising rather than exacerbating tension amongst staff and students, for students are enabled to maintain the fiction that the academics are more on their "side" than are the governors.

However, the immediate effect of the Governors' statement on this occasion was to ensure that whatever support the occupation would previously have attracted, it would now be overwhelmingly popular. The union council came under great pressure to re-open the issue yet again; a minority of its members went over to the revolutionaries. Although I well understood the reasons for the reaction, this did not affect my original view of the occupation, and in any case I still believed we had been cheated of our legitimate majority in the large union meeting. If the union vote against the occupation had been allowed to stand, the authorities would not have needed to act. We stood firm, but it became clear that the progress made since spring 1967 in rebuilding trust and co-operation within the School was rapidly being dissipated. The tensions of the earlier crisis were too close in memory to withstand a blow of these proportions. It would probably have been better if the matter had been allowed to rest when the revolutionaries gained their initial majority at the emergency union meeting; again I had angered them by inciting opposition against them.

However, the pressures which we had exerted upon them had one extremely positive result where the safety of the School was concerned. The leading faction of the occupation was determined to ensure that no damage occurred, and that the School buildings were vacated in a cleaner state than when they had been occupied. Since several elements within the occupation had very different aspirations, it is possible that it was the determination by the occupiers to show up such critics as myself as alarmist which provided the major constraint upon their behaviour.

The occupation had gone ahead, and Adams's closure of

the School had proved purely formal. The occupiers' public relations exercise of cleaning the buildings was extremely successful; the following week a censure motion on the union council was passed at a union meeting. The union also adopted an extremely militant policy which amounted to daring the governors to come out and fight.

What was now to be done? We had hopelessly lost the initiative to the left, and the union seemed set on recreating March 1967. To regain the initiative would involve some sort of action by the union council which would divert attention. But only one course seemed available to us: resignation. Five of us joined to prepare a lengthy statement of resignation which would set down our view of the crisis facing the School and at the same time try to force students and staff alike to think deeply about the direction in which we were heading.

The statement received a surprising amount of attention outside the School, and internally the move had, at least temporarily, the desired effect. First, it threw the revolutionaries into a quandary; they had now been directly challenged to take part in an election, a course they had previously avoided. They decided to stand, and we also prepared a list of candidates; it would be a straight contest between the revolutionary view of the future of the LSE and that of what had come to be called the "moderates".

In the closing two weeks of my time in office we had a further and unexpected victory; despite all that had gone before, we were successful in getting the union to approve the detailed policy on student representation on which I had been working. At last both academic staff and students had approaches on this original issue that were within negotiable reach of each other. The elections, which attracted unprecedented interest within the college, saw the election of the "moderate" candidates. The new president was Francis Keohane, a good friend of mine and a fellow Labour Party man. Within a month the moderates had pulled back a long way from the débâcle of Vietnam weekend.

The closing weeks of the winter term continued in this direction. The only major incident was the Oration Day lecture, which was to be given by Professor Hugh Trevor-Roper, the historian. Some students had discovered some extraordinary eulogies of the Greek colonels' regime by Trevor-Roper, and a campaign was soon in train to have the meeting disrupted on the pattern that had been set at several other universities. Added incitement to the students was provided by the fact that the seats in the Old Theatre where the lecture was to be given had been reserved for members of the Court of Governors. A limited number of tickets were available to students in the gallery. In the normal course of events of course, few students ever bothered to attend this sole example of traditional pageantry at the LSE. This year, however, it was planned that students should occupy the Old Theatre before the Governors could take their places, and prevent the lecture from being given.

But within the LSE student body there was strong resistance to the idea of disrupting meetings addressed by outside speakers, and in the days before Oration Day, this pressure made itself felt. The plans changed to occupying the Old Theatre and forcing Trevor-Roper to answer questions about Greece. Needless to say, an unprecedented number of students gathered in the Old Theatre. Trevor-Roper entered the crowded hall with the new chairman of the Court, Lord Robbins, and the Director, to be confronted with the student demands. Robbins said that he was pleased to see so many students at the Oration Day, that the governors had been accommodated in another room connected by loudspeakers to the Old Theatre, and that a second lecture theatre had been booked for a session after the oration, when Trevor-Roper would answer questions on Greece. As for a further demand that Robbins himself answer questions about LSE from the students, he would be delighted to do so at a meeting the following term.

The oration took place in peace; isolated heckling of Trevor-Roper's criticisms of Marxism were hushed by the mass of the audience; Robbins received a personal ovation at the end; and groups of revolutionaries held an urgent inquest on what had gone wrong. It had, in particular, been a

78

surprising victory for Robbins. For the first and only time the authorities had responded to a student challenge with tact, openness and good humour. A small step of progress had been made towards repairing the great breach that existed between the authorities and a substantial section of the student body. The term ended peacefully.

But the new-found optimism was a fragile plant indeed. The far left had tasted blood on the Vietnam issue and were aware of the reservoirs of support on which they could, in a crisis, draw. It will have been noted that the internal issues of representation and the like had been entirely dropped by the militants, although in such areas of School life as departmental staff-student meetings they could still be found ardently calling for the abolition of all distinctions between staff and students and the government of departments by general assemblies of all their "members". The main interest of the revolutionaries now rested in building a "red base"[7] at LSE: a place where they could recruit members to a revolutionary movement and where they could stage prototype revolutionary actions. The concern was with wide political issues, but an important aspect of this was the demonstration that the university was inextricably linked with a variety of exploitative evils. The Greece issue was an instance of this, and in the spring term the focus of attention shifted to southern Africa, where it had all started with the original agitation against Adams's appointment.

LENT TERM, 1969

The Commonwealth Prime Ministers Conference was to take place in January, and Rhodesia was to be an important topic on the agenda. There was pressure within the union before the end of the Christmas term for a teach-in on Rhodesia to co-incide with the conference. Keohane spent his Christmas vacation working on such a teach-in, with co-operation from the Director. The Socialist Society also planned for the teach-in, and characteristically the direction of their plans was an attempt to discover whether the LSE had any investments in

79

Rhodesian or South African firms. They also learned that during the early weeks of the coming term representatives of certain companies would be coming to the School to hold recruiting interviews with students; some of these firms had business connections with South Africa.

An "Agitator" pamphlet was prepared on all these matters for the beginning of term. The teach-in was to last from January 8–10. The question of the School's involvement was raised when Adams addressed the teach-in on the first day. He was confronted with demands that the LSE should publish a list of its investments and of any holdings it had in Rhodesia and South Africa;* that LSE Governors should divest themselves of directorships in such companies or, alternatively, resign from the Court; and that companies with South African holdings should not be allowed on LSE premises to interview students for jobs. It was also said that if these demands were not met, direct action of an unspecified kind would be taken to enforce them. Adams agreed to address the teach-in again on January 10 to deal with the questions raised.

On January 10 the meeting was crowded, and Adams refuted some of the allegations made and refused to take action on the others. He left the meeting discussing the issue. Towards the end of the evening's discussion, they decided that they wanted Adams to appear before them again, and sent a delegation to fetch him. He refused, so they decided to bring him from his office, and a large section of the meeting surged through the School buildings and up the stairs towards the administrative building, where they were confronted by firmly locked iron fire-doors. The drawbridge was up. In their anger the students sought an alternative victim, and a few yards away stood the invitingly open doors of the

* Adams complied with this request, and the information revealed that the School owned £250 of gold shares in the South African firm of De Beers. It had no connections with Rhodesia. However, the Socialist Society drew attention to the School's involvements with Shell International, which they alleged (without any evidence) had been supplying oil illegally to Rhodesia.

senior common room. It was duly invaded, and a couple of hundred students embarked on a spontaneous teach-in-cum-sit-in to the amusement and wonder of the staff in the room. Meeting no resistance, the students became bored and went home at about 10.30 pm. A large general assembly convened the following Monday, but little transpired. It had been hoped by some that the meeting would transfer itself to the administrative building, and guards had been stationed at the fire doors to prevent the authorities having them closed. Their efforts were not necessary.

It may have been the experience of meeting the fire doors that soon afterwards dramatically turned students' attention away from the South African shares to the matter of the gates. We have encountered at several points in this narrative the inability of an LSE protest to remain fixed on one issue, but this sudden dropping of the South African shares in favour of an onslaught on the ludicrous issue of the gates was the most blatant example of this tendency, and was later to become a source of bitter regret to some of the revolutionary leaders and the cause of fatal divisions within the revolutionary movement. The LSE crisis of Lent term 1969 reads like a bizarre quadruple fugue, with the subject of the gates eventually riding above the other themes to dominate the finale. But we have still only introduced three of the subjects: the South African shares involvement, the recruitment by firms with South African connections and the gates. A fourth issue, closely connected with the gates, was introduced by a report of the General Purposes Committee of the Academic Board.

This report was the product of the events of October 25–27, and a demand expressed at that time by the board that the School prepare itself more adequately in the future for this kind of emergency. The committee had addressed itself to the question of the rights and responsibilities of members of staff in the event of such crises, and it proceeded to spell out these obligations as it saw them. It gave advice on how to deal with the disruption of lectures and examinations by students, and included such items as a duty on members of staff to identify students they observed taking part in obstructive protests, and recognition that in "exceptional circumstances" staff may be justified in "the use of force" against protesting students. It went on to spell out in detail the general responsibilities of academics where student protests were concerned. It was short-sighted of the committee not to realise the kind of reaction there would be among the student body and many of the staff to such a document. It contributed greatly to the general atmosphere of mistrust and paranoia that was beginning to permeate the life of the School, and which could only be to the advantage of one group; the revolutionaries.

(It is worth noting that much of the pressure for an explicit statement of rights and duties had come from the radicals on the staff, who called for explicitness and for matters to be spelt out in detail. They seemed to forget that things left vague can be far less confining. The GPC report really did little more than spell out what would evidently occur anyway; it was obvious that many members of staff would willingly report students disrupting the School, while those members of staff who would not be disposed so to act would not be any more likely to do so as a result of the GPC report. Such attempts as the GPC report are almost certain to accompany large-scale disruptions in institutions where some members are straining at the limits of the unwritten rules and tacit agreements that normally make it possible for life to be apparently regulated.)

In the event, the Academic Board substantially changed the GPC's proposals. But they contributed very much to the general unhealthy state of staff-student relations that was being cultivated by the issue of the gates. The combination of Southern Africa and internal tensions was beginning to create that heady and passionate atmosphere so crucial to a successful protest movement.

The first major discussion of the gates in the union occurred at a meeting at which Lord Robbins addressed the students and answered questions. This took place the following Friday. Unlike his encounter over the Trevor-Roper affair, the meeting was not a successful one. Nearly all the discussion had been on the issue of the South African involvement, and the atmosphere between Robbins and the union had grown strained. But towards the end of the meeting attention turned to the gates. The gates in question were a series of rather ugly black iron gates, similar in design to lift gates, which had been erected at strategic points throughout the School buildings by the authorities. They had in fact been erected for some time, and notices explaining the erection had been posted in the previous term, during my presidency. They had however aroused no major interest at all. In essence all they did was to provide for the LSE what geography and architecture have provided as a matter of course for virtually every other university: the physical separation of its constituent parts, enabling some to be opened while others remained closed. Since the LSE was increasing its activities of hiring out lecture theatres for conferences, and allowing various types of outsiders into the college for set purposes, the policy could be defended on those grounds. It was also clear, of course, that the gates would be useful in the event of a sit-in by students in order to contain the "area of occupation". Indeed, most sit-ins at other universities had implicitly accepted such constraints by making the target of an occupation a particular building, usually the administrative building. The authorities' fears on this matter had been particularly increased by the fears of "Vietnam weekend".

(It is a reflection on the strength of conservatism among even the most dedicated revolutionaries that measures of change always give rise to defensive cries on behalf of previously unheard-of rights. In this case many people suddenly cherished deeply the right to have a college in which one part of the building was not separated from another by means of gates. The gates were eventually replaced with a smaller number of more handsome wooden doors that blended better with the surrounding design; this produced no wave of protest. Perhaps student militants have a finer sense of aesthetics than is usually credited.)

Since little had been done through orthodox channels, the way was clear for the proponents of direct action to take the initiative. The gates would have to be taken down by direct, mass student action. This attitude demonstrated complete rejection of the notion that the LSE authorities had any rights of control and order whatsoever. The militants were now operating very clearly with a model of the School that saw themselves as the sole arbiters of its destiny, and the only group with a right to decide within it. Gates erected by the authorities were to be treated in the same way that, say, the Metropolitan Police would treat a barricade erected across the Strand by LSE students.

Several large meetings of students discussed the issue. Sometimes the meetings would be "general assemblies", loosely spontaneous gatherings set up by the Socialist Society in opposition to the students' union and governed by no constitution or any of the rules that normally govern fair debate. It was yet another example of the opposition between spontaneous, unstructured groupings, and bureaucratic, legalistic ones. But at other times the union itself would meet, and here the militants faced the usual reluctance of the LSE student body to act rashly. Many students wanted an attempt at negotiation, and did not like the suspicion of violence implied in the threat to take the gates down. Others feared for the response of the authorities and disliked the prospect of yet another term of disruption.

The militants countered these arguments partly by asserting their challenge to the legitimacy of the authorities, and partly by an intriguing symbolism. We have noted before how the new left sees "authority" as an undistinguished monolith, there being no essential difference between the LSE Court of Governors, the American State Department, the Zurich bankers or the Kremlin. The gates were an act of authority; the possibilities of interpretation were infinite and advantage was taken of them. Nicholas Bateson, a lecturer in social psychology later dismissed from the School for his part in the events, said that tearing down the gates was required of us if we were to show proper solidarity with the Africans in Rhodesia, the guerrillas in Thailand and the Arabs in Palestine (sic). Robin Blackburn, a lecturer in sociology also later dismissed, said that the gates were the material expression of class oppression. The majority remained unmoved; they asked for negotiations.

The divisions on this matter were not simply those between "moderates" and "militants". A published narrative of these events by two American radicals who had been deeply involved in them, Paul Hoch and Vic Schoenbach,[8] makes clear the emergence of deep divisions between themselves and the Marxist establishment of the Socialist Society. According to these authors, the Marxists were extremely wary of taking militant action, preferring a more academic approach and also having no patience with student activities which were little related to the wider class struggle. The Hoch-Schoenbach book is essentially a testament fot the "act now, think later" school of radicalism.* It is in fact this approach which marks a deep gulf between today's young militants and yesterday's Marxists. An important source of the quictism of the British student revolt is the continuing influence of the older tradition.

The union met for a final time on a Friday afternoon. Negotiations with Adams had resulted in some changes on the gates policy, but these were not enough for the militants. The audience at the meeting was considerably smaller than that for previous discussions of this issue. The militants said they would not feel confident unless they had 300 votes behind them; they also pointed out that all that was required to take down the gates was a screw-driver. They received a majority, but not 300 votes. A large section of the militants left the hall and rushed through the School to attack the

---

* Hoch and Schoenbach seem obsessed with two different opponents. First is the Secretary of State for Education and Science for saying that the LSE militants were a small minority not concerned with academic study and only interested in disruptive activity; second they reproach the Socialist Society for not being prepared to take actions not backed by a majority, for being too concerned with an academic approach to revolution, and for not appreciating the value of disruptive activity for its own sake.

gates with sledgehammers, crow-bars and pick-axes.* There were angry scenes as members of the academic staff tried to hinder their progress. It was exactly one week short of the second anniversary of the death of Mr Edward Poole, the school porter.

Adams was informed of what was occurring, and, fearing for the safety of both persons and buildings, summoned the police. He decided to close the School at the end of the evening. By the time the police arrived, after unconscionable delays, it was all over. But some of the militants had been foolish enough to go to the union bar. Police surrounded the building, and students were brought up from the bar in small groups to be identified by members of the academic staff. Those "identified" were taken to Bow Street police station, where a demonstration took place that led to further arrests. This whole disagreeable episode did much to create a gulf between members of the staff and a large number of students. The epithet "academic spy" became attached to those members of staff who had taken part in the process. If the police had acted faster and taken the students while in the act of destroying the gates, the School would have been spared this source of antagonism which soured the rest of the year, resulting in an excess of neurosis on all sides.

Throughout the crisis of 1967 an essential atmosphere of friendliness between staff and students had survived; this was not to be in 1969. In 1967 one of the administration's failures had been its unwillingness to communicate with students on terms other than that of high authority to its subjects; in 1969 Adams appealed to his students and was rebuffed by them. That was the extent to which attitudes among staff, students and authorities had changed in two years.

Now the added factor was the closure of the School. This was crucial to the left's ability to mobilise effective protest.

---

* Hoch and Schoenbach boast of the contrast between the screwdrivers of the union discussion and the pickaxes of the deed. It is justified on the grounds that students' fears had to be allayed.[9]

On previous occasions the area around the Old Theatre had formed a centre of gravity for the protest movement; from there had been generated the mood of the movement. Now the students were in the diaspora, with no access to the temple and the holy city. The first need was therefore a building, and the University of London Union building, a place of resort for all students of the university, was booked for a meeting the following Monday. Thanks to press publicity, a vast audience of students arrived, and adopted a defiant stand towards the authorities; it was clear who was to be blamed for the closure. Later in the day the building was rudely seized from its guardians, other student groups wishing to use it were thrown out and their meetings broken up, and the revolutionaries adopted it as their headquarters where they could carry on the ritual that had originated in 1967 of long declamatory meetings lasting far into the night.

But considerable disagreement existed among the occupying forces. According to Hoch and Schoenbach[10] the Socialist Society establishment was responsible for proposing a peaceful march to the LSE that afternoon; the march broke up at the School and students went home. This meant that only a small number of LSE students were available to take over the ULU building. This had two implications. First, from the start the occupation was dominated by outsiders; and second, there was considerable acrimony among different segments of the occupiers.

Within a few days the number of outsiders was so large that the LSE contingent was a minority in its own protest. This, together with threats of rude eviction from aggrieved and potentially vicious students of the University of London, led to a feeling of insecurity among the occupiers. Although they continued to stay in the building and hold meetings, they ceased the attempt to hold it as "revolutionary property". In fact, it is possible that the affair would shortly afterwards have expired, had the LSE not then taken out injunctions against 13 persons involved in the "gates" incident, restraining them from entering the LSE, and sent Blackburn and Bateson notice that they would be subject to disciplinary action. This rescued the revolutionaries from dissension and boredom and ensured that they stayed in action.

As the days progressed the most extraordinary position was reached. The LSE was scattered throughout Bloomsbury. Many students worked at home, but lectures and classes were being held in various buildings of the university. The revolutionaries held the ULU building, and Keohane established his head-quarters in a well-concealed room deep inside an uninhabited part of University College. (Originally he had occupied a more open room at UC, but had been driven out by a group of militants.) Keohane had resigned when the students decided to tear down the gates, but had to remain in office until a successor could be elected. Although thoroughly disillusioned with the students he was meant to represent, he did what he could over the coming weeks to find a meeting point between the authorities and the mass of students, but without success. A further group of students, calling themselves the "moderates", had set up residence in the Catholic Chaplaincy of the University of London, where under the shadow of a huge crucifix they tried to plot opposition to the revolution and rally the faithful.

But of more importance to our present concerns than these bizarre happenings was the state reached in the growth of a student movement and its relationship to college authorities. On paper the position of the latter was strong. The militants had been deprived of the all-important LSE base, and Adams was sending a series of letters to each student's home address (subsequently known as the "Dear Student" letters) explaining at length what had happened and why he had acted as he did, and calling for a condemnation of the use of violence in the course of student protest. Thus the individual student, it was hoped, sitting at home far from the heady atmosphere of the LSE, would read the letters, see the sense of the authorities' case, and rally round.

The School's approach was highly intelligent. Adams was clearly seeking to gain student consent in drawing the boundaries of student protest. I think it was very important to him as director that he be able to know of certain constraints that protesting students would impose on their own actions, so that he could then respond to various kinds of protest within a broadly political context, not needing to respond with alarm to every outbreak. Adams had privately drawn the line at the use of violence, and he had been greatly dismayed that this line had now been crossed. He sought an assurance from the rest of the student body that they would back his constraint on violence.

It was to this end that the first "Dear Student" letter was directed; it was closely linked to plans for a vast union meeting summoned at Friends' House, Euston, by Keohane. Over 1,500 people attended the lengthy session. The verdict of this meeting could not be considered by anyone to be that of an unrepresentative minority; the total student body at LSE was 3,200, of whom half were graduate students who rarely took any interest in college affairs.

Three broad factions faced the meeting, seeking its support. On one extreme the Socialist Society sought virtually a declaration of war on the School; the previous day the authorities had taken out injunctions in the High Court to prevent several of the leading militants from re-entering the School, and the left was angry and somewhat fearful. Second, a group of students fell short of the militants' demands for immediate direct action, but nevertheless put the blame for the closure on the authorities, opposed all discipline on those responsible for the destruction of the gates, and signally failed to respond to Adams's call for a condemnation of violence. Finally, a group of us called for a condemnation of violence, dissociated ourselves from the action in tearing down the gates, but sought to pledge the union to ensuring that the inevitable disciplinary action was carried out fairly and justly.

By a wide majority the second group won. In a way it was also a victory for the militants, for the two sides were not divided on any fundamental matters. The only group defeated were those of us who sought to respond to Adams's appeal. Despite the absence from the LSE buildings, despite the violence, despite the "Dear Student" letter, despite the size of the meeting, the students of the LSE had failed to respond to Adams's appeal. They had refused to condemn violence at a meeting held in the headquarters of Quakerism. Like the student response to the Court's action over Vietnam weekend, the depth of the weakness of the LSE authorities was profound indeed.

One can produce many explanations as to why the students of the School responded in this way, and all of them are valid to some extent; the motives of a large bunch of people are bound to be complex and diverse. But underlying them all I suspect the explanation lies in the myth of the "average student". It is always assumed in discussion of the student problem that there is a minority of noisy rebellious students, and a vast majority of quiet, loyal, reasonable ones. It is further assumed that this reasonableness is the result of a degree of political maturity and sophistication. This is the myth. In everyday life the "average man" is not expected to make decisions of political sophistication; he lacks both the desire and opportunity to do so. It is only in the myths of mass participation that every man is his own politician, and it is an instance of the new left's success in propagating this myth that the university authorities should themselves seek support from the mass student body and expect to be able to receive such support.

I shall not here anticipate the argument to be deployed in Chapter Five, except to point out that in a crisis the "average student" will take the course of action easiest to him. At Friends' House it was easier to take the course of supporting colleagues than to appreciate the finer points of the director's appeal. A couple of weeks after the re-opening of the School the situation was reversed, and the students' behaviour then is also explicable once we appreciate the myth of the average student. It is to these events that we now turn.

After three weeks of closure the School re-opened, and we returned from the Exile. The revolutionaries celebrated with a carnival parade, taking their text from Lenin ("Revolution is the festival of the oppressed"). Eagerly returning to the Old Theatre, they ensured that a union meeting was soon organised where they could enact the expected ritual of denunciation and expressions of solidarity.

But it was to remain mere ritual. The union, and according to Hoch and Schoenbach[11] the Marxist leadership, were unprepared to go beyond verbal expressions of support. Calls for an occupation were defeated. Meanwhile the School was preparing its disciplinary action. The injunctions were being modified,* but the disciplinary hearing on Bateson had already taken place and the verdict was awaited. The left were now in the position which had been previously occupied by the union establishment: they had a tacit majority support, but were unable to call upon this support to take positive action. Appropriately, it was at this point that members of the Socialist Society won the bulk of places on the union council.† The revolution was being undermined by its own success.

It will be argued in later chapters that the kind of model of action provided by the new left is essentially transitory, dependent very much on a flush of emotion and sudden dislocation of normal life. When the matter becomes protracted, it is difficult to sustain this atmosphere and spread the movement beyond the confines of the inner circle of revolutionaries. At the LSE some members of this inner circle retreated to appropriately small-scale actions, allegedly based on the model of "guerrilla warfare". They would make little forays to attack the offices of members of staff, and similar activities characteristic of the younger classes of a badly-behaved secondary school.

Matters within the college were still serious. The School continued to try to renew its injunctions, but the "bourgeois"

---

* Except in the case of Hoch, who claims he was summarily "expelled" from the LSE.[12] Since he was never a student of the School, it is difficult to see how this could have been the case.

† The exceptions, curiously, were the key positions of president and general secretary. The new president, Chris Pryce, had been, like myself, a chairman of the LSE Labour Society. It is curious that throughout the years of crisis there was only one break in the continuity of a Labour president: and he had been a Conservative. Pryce was eventually succeeded by his brother Gareth.

courts came to the aid of the revolutionaries; this was of course interpreted as an instance of the cunning of the ruling class and its mystifications. But it was becoming evident that High Court injunctions were clumsy weapons for a university to use against its students. There are certain types of behaviour which may seem intolerable offences within a university community, but which cannot appear particularly outrageous to a judge who daily observes a procession of human vice and violence. If a university considers that closer ties bind its members than the simple ties between citizens of the same country, then it is appropriate that the university have its own rules and disciplinary procedures. But at the LSE the internal machinery had been discredited and was known to be inadequate, so the authorities turned to the outside courts in the vain hope of acquiring an effective legitimacy for sanctions which they could not command themselves. The student left could hardly complain; it is generally the position of revolutionary students that (i) the university should be a community with special membership bonds but that (ii) there should be no sanctions over the members apart from those of the general law.

In the wake of the renewed attempts at discipline there was a further attempt at introducing a resolution for occupation in the union; again the union preferred to offer verbal solidarity, but a tiny group of "disillusioned moderates" carried on a strange vigil outside the Old Theatre, sitting there doing their academic work, for several days.

But on March 7 something more dramatic occurred. Criminal summonses had been taken out by the Director of Public Prosecutions against eight students and two lecturers; they were accused of committing wilful damage on the night of the gates. On March 10 the union at last approved a motion calling for an occupation, which began that night. But the material support given to it was less than the number of votes it had received. It was only able to keep going through a large infusion of the usual outsiders. If Adams had been deserted by his students at the large meeting in Friends' House it was now the revolutionaries' turn to experience betrayal.

In past sit-ins the Marxist leadership had shown an ability to control the behaviour of more extreme fringe elements; on this occasion they failed. Many of the occupiers were embittered by the desertion of the majority of students and, as we have seen before, an important element on the left was challenging the strategy of the Marxists. Outsiders added a further element of unpredictability, and the small numbers involved in the occupation meant that there was no solid mass of passive supporters to give stability. Earlier that week a leaflet had been widely circulated by the anarchists, calling for acts of "creative vandalism" to be committed against the School.

During the night of the occupation the "guerrilla bands" set to work. Extraordinary slogans, spray-painted, covered virtually every wall and every door of members of staff who had been involved in disciplinary action against students (the unmistakable trade mark of students from the University of Essex), and the door of Dr Percy Cohen, Dean of Undergraduate studies,* was forced open, paint spilled over his desk, examination papers being prepared for the following summer stolen, and minutes of certain School committees which had discussed the crisis were taken and subsequently published. In the early hours of the morning the split within the revolutionary movement could be seen at its most blatant; the old Marxist leaders of the LSE revolution were cleaning and tidying the invaded office and scrubbing slogans from the walls.

News of the disruptions of the night disaffected many potential sympathisers of the occupation, and although it staggered on for a further night it was greatly weakened and spluttered to a halt. In 1967 the Easter vacation had rescued a successful sit-in from quarrels between "moderates" and "militants". In 1969 it saved an unsuccessful occupation from quarrels between Marxists and "creative vandals".

---

* That militant students should have made a special target of Cohen was one of the major injustices committed at the School during the year. His only offence appears to have been a willingness to engage in articulate argument with them.

93

The British student movement had had its chance to engage in a full-blooded disruption on the model established in various other western countries, but had found its inhibitions too strong.

SUMMER TERM, 1969

On April 18, three days before the start of the summer term, it was announced that Bateson and Blackburn would be dismissed for their approbation of the destruction of the gates. There could be no appeal.

This was a far more important measure of discipline than had been imposed on Adelstein and Bloom in 1967; it shocked more of the staff than had that incident, and it came at the end of a long succession of troubles. However, it was to lead to a very different pattern of protest. Students returned to the School from the vacation to find that the revolutionaries had called for a strike and a boycott of all activities of the School. This was not a "passive" boycott of the kind we had organised in 1966, for it involved proclaiming a state of siege against the School. Lorry drivers bringing food, coal, beer, laundry and (with puzzling frequency) yoghurt, were "persuaded" by various means from delivering their wares. There were occasionally ugly scenes as van drivers tried to beat the picket line.

Similarly, inside the School there were attempts at disrupting classes and lectures by trying to start "discussions" within them of the crisis. The little teams of "guerrilla fighters" continued to do their work. Now that revolutionaries controlled the union council and hence union facilities, they were able to cover the School with their leaflets and other activities. Once or twice a grossly amplified record-player was set up at a strategic point in order to render it impossible even to work in the library.

But although the college was in a state of virtual chaos, active participation in the disruption was limited to a small if ubiquitous group. The nature of the activities did not facilitate mass participation, but, more important, the will to

94

be taken into a rapidly escalating protest movement was lacking. A student revolt is most successful when there is a rapid succession of events building up to a crisis, and where the revolutionary leadership can successfully innovate activities which appear to satisfy widespread anxieties. In 1969 the crisis was too protracted and the activities of the now divided leadership lacked co-ordination. Boredom and *déjà vu* are the final enemies of this type of revolution.

The Academic Board took up aspects of the case of Blackburn and Bateson and an appeal was agreed.* Most of the court charges for malicious damage were eventually dropped, but the School did take internal disciplinary action against a few students who had been involved in the later disruptions, although in most instances the punishments were token. The only other event of note during the summer term was the visit of the Select Committee of the House of Commons who had been touring universities and other institutions of higher education in order to study student relations (see page 123). A few days beforehand the Committee had had its meeting broken up at the University of Essex, and they experienced the same fate at the LSE.

We have suggested at several points in the course of this narrative why the revolt grew or declined in strength at particular points, and it is not necessary to summarise these now. The most interesting aspect of the LSE story at this stage was the decline of the protest movement, which we have tried to make explicable within a frame of reference which will be examined in more detail in later chapters.

As the summer term progressed, two further pressures reinforced the in-built tendencies to decline: the imminence of examinations and the real threat of disciplinary action. The protest had been thrust into failure at its potentially strongest point since the early stirrings of 1965–66. The authorities of

---

* Blackburn took advantage of the offer of an appeal, and an elaborately constructed tribunal of outside academics and lawyers heard his case and rejected it during the summer vacation. A third member of the staff, Lawrence Harris, appeared before an internal tribunal at the start of the new academic year, but no action was taken against him.

the School were grossly unpopular. At some points in the Lent term the revolutionaries could probably claim the support of a majority of the student body. And now victory was being denied them. In the midst of inter-revolutionary vituperation, tense and strained staff-student relationships, and a general weariness and boredom, the student protest at the LSE, and the summer term, choked to a halt.

REFERENCES

1. London School of Economics and Political Science, Report of Committee on the Machinery of Government, 1968
2. *ibid* (extracts from the Minority Report have been published in Atkinson, R., "Aspects of Student Power" (in Crouch, C. (ed), *Students Today*, Fabian Society, 1968) and in Atkinson, R., "The Academic Situation" (in Nagal, J. (ed), *Student Power*, 1969)
3. *ibid*, Minority Report, Part III, p 4
4. *ibid*, Minority Report, Part III
5. *ibid*, Majority Report, p 26
6. Fawthrop, T., *Education or Examination*, Radical Students Alliance, 1968, p 65
7. *New Left Review*, No. 53, 1969
8. Hoch, P. and Schoenbach, V., *LSE: The Natives Are Restless*, 1969, ch 6
9. *ibid*, p 63
10. *ibid*, p 76 *et seq*
11. *ibid*, p 128 *et seq*
12. *ibid*, p 124

CHAPTER FOUR

Student Revolt in Britain, 1966–69

Student revolt in Britain has been distinguished from that in other countries of the western world, not to mention Japan, by its quietness and passivity. The extent of violence and extremity of actions have been limited. As we saw in the closing sections of Chapter Three, this causes great frustration to American radicals who have come to Britain hoping to share in activities similar to those in their own country. French revolutionary students, for all their stress on breaking free from the past and on the irrelevance of history, can be seen as part of a tradition of French political activity stretching back from 1848 through the 1830s to 1789. Similarly the quietism of the British revolt reflects a national tradition. The restrained virtues of English political culture have suffused even our most militant rebels.

However, the student revolt has not been insignificant in this country. As I shall suggest in my final chapter, its characteristic philosophy can be seen in a far more general context of cultural and religious developments: it has produced a literature which has aroused widespread interest; and it has influenced the perspectives of a very wide range of young people in colleges and universities. It is likely that the extent of influence of the new left goes way beyond its simple ability to foment particular outbreaks of protest. But in this chapter our attention will be mainly concentrated on such outbreaks. It is when a general set of attitudes reaches sufficient strength to impel action that we can discover its most significant concerns. The events at the LSE in the winter of 1966, carrying on until the spring of 1967, were the first outbreaks of direct action by students in recent times in

Britain. In the USA, the Berkeley campus of the University of California had been in chaos since 1964, and the revolt had spread to other universities there. In West Germany, particularly in Berlin, there had been disturbances since the establishment of the big coalition of the Christian and Social Democrats. In Japan the Zengakuren had already established a bloody record of street fighting.

But the LSE affair was the first event of its kind in Britain, and it had covered a sprawling confusion of issues. Rhodesia, student participation, a critique of "bourgeois" education, an attack on the "capitalist" university – indeed the whole range of issues which were to appear sporadically and sometimes in isolation at a number of other institutions were present in the original LSE dispute. There was one exception to this: the LSE revolutionaries had not produced a theory of imposing restrictions on the freedom of speech of their political opponents, although this was later to become an important theme for their contemporaries in several other places.

For some time campus revolt did not spread from the LSE, although a hint of future attitudes was the formation of the Radical Students Alliance early in 1967, originally consisting of a fairly wide range of left-wing views, but mainly concerned with changing the "moderate" and politically orthodox style of the National Union of Students. The first outbreak elsewhere occurred in December 1967, when students at the Regent Street Polytechnic and the Holborn College of Law and Commerce demonstrated and briefly sat-in on the issue of student representation. It is notable that both these colleges are in London, and indeed, in the neighbourhood of the LSE. In the following month students at Aston University (in Birmingham) disrupted their institution in support of similar demands. They held a brief sit-in in the administrative block to try to force the authorities to accept student representation. The university established a committee to examine this and related questions.

A protest of somewhat different kind occurred at the University of Edinburgh, where Malcolm Muggeridge was

98

involved in great controversy with certain groups of students following his refusal, as rector, to represent their views on birth control before the university authorities. Although various issues became involved in this dispute, it is possible to identify a demand by students for a direct form of student representation which the ancient and unique Scottish rectorial system does not provide. The rector is under no obligation to speak for policies approved by the students.

Students at the University of Leicester had been preparing proposals for student representation which involved a modest level of participation on certain major committees of the university. (The degree of representation demanded was in fact considerably less than that being proposed at about the same time by the authorities at the LSE, and which was about to be rejected by the student body there.) The Leicester administration refused to concede, and a large number of students at this previously most apolitical university found themselves sitting in the administration building. After some days the union decided to call off the sit-in following an offer of further talks by the university. The debate, which decided to accept the agreement, saw an overwhelming defeat of the revolutionary left in a discussion that was notable for the strength and fierceness of its passions, which seemed out of all proportion to the nature of the students' own unambitious demands. This is a frequent and important characteristic of student protests. The initial demands are for something on the lines of membership of committees. This is the only way, at least initially, that the demand for "participation" can be given tangible organisational form. But the expectations linked to this idea of participation, the anger felt at its denial, and the way in which both the demand and the means of protest adopted to attain it are associated with a whole range of other political sentiments, are reasonable indications that discussion of numbers of students to sit on committees has really very little to do with the whole affair.

It was in the same month – February – as the Leicester protest that the first examples of what was to become a new factor in the student protest emerged. These were vehement,

99

possibly violent, demonstrations against visiting outside speakers to the university of whom groups of students disapproved. This element had been potentially present at the LSE when the idea of using direct action to prevent Walter Adams taking up his appointment had been discussed; but it was never followed up in practice. The first person to suffer from this form of protest was an official of the US Embassy who was covered in red paint when he visited the University of Sussex to talk about Vietnam. Disciplinary action was taken against the individuals concerned with, apparently, the approval of the student body. This is the only major incident of student disruption at Sussex, which has an elaborate system of disciplinary procedure involving proctors (youthful members of the academic staff) and students, with a clear and explicit structure of appeals and a wide-ranging brief that covers, besides normal disciplinary matters, such issues as disputes between students and their landladies. In this way discipline seems to have a different image at Sussex than in less fortunate institutions, where it still appears as a remote and magisterial arbitrary authority.

Shortly afterwards in a similar incident at the University of Essex, two Conservative MPs (Mr Enoch Powell and Mr Antony Buck) were molested when leaving the university after addressing a meeting. Essex revolutionaries pride themselves on the fact that they discovered Mr Powell's views on coloured immigrants over a year before he chose to publicise them on national scale. This was to be but the first flexing of muscles by students at Essex, who rival LSE for the chronic state of their revolt, although, interestingly, it has always taken a different form.

In March several events of this kind took place. They appeared temporarily to replace student participation as a demand. The Secretary of State for Education and Science, Mr Patrick Gordon Walker, was shouted down when trying to address a meeting at the University of Manchester. This led to the suspension of two students, which in turn led to new protests. This did not, however, lead to a major confrontation. Students at Oxford threatened to duck another minister, Mr James Callaghan, in a pond. And at Cambridge the Secretary of State for Defence, Mr Denis Healey, had great difficulty in reaching a meeting because of student demonstrators. A more sophisticated exercise by Cambridge radicals was a "free university" which attracted considerable attention.

March was also the month of the first violent encounter between police and demonstrators outside the US Embassy in Grosvenor Square. The issue, of course, was Vietnam. Although this was not entirely a student event, it fitted into the pattern that was being set by the new student left in many places: a pattern of recourse to semi-violent action, not through irresponsible hooliganism but because of a definite belief in the theoretical and moral appropriateness of such a course of action. It was part of the developing ideology of opposition to institutional politics and the use of established channels for registering dissent which was growing up parallel with and related to the demand for student participation in the running of universities.

This developing trend of activity caused great concern to the National Union of Students, partly because they feared that their activities on behalf of students would be handicapped by the bad "image" which was being acquired, and partly because their own standing within the student movement, and that of their kind of politics, were being undermined by the militant action and the increasing adherence to it of groups of students. At about this time the Government announced that it would cut by half original proposals for an increase in students' grants. The NUS leadership took the opportunity to organise their own demonstration in Trafalgar Square, at which they also found occasion to attack the new militancy. They launched an extended campaign on the grants issue, but it seemed to become inextricably involved in Vietnam campaigns, in the minds of both militant students and the media.

By this time student demonstrations had become a topic of considerable interest. The success with which the notion of direct action had been accepted by various student groups can be seen from the fact that at the University of York it was possible to organise a short sit-in on the mundane problem of school meals.

SUMMER TERM, 1968

At the beginning of the summer term, usually a quiet one in student affairs because of the proximity of examinations, there were new protests. At the University of Leeds Mr Patrick Wall MP and his wife were subjected to mobbing when he addressed a meeting there. The issue at stake was race, for Wall had become noted for his extreme right-wing views on both coloured immigration and Rhodesia. Race has proved to be the sparking point for several student demonstrations concerned with non-university issues, and this was the period of the aftermath of Enoch Powell's infamous speech.

Race became, or seemed to become, an internal issue in a problem at the Enfield College of Technology. The authorities had decided to reduce their intake of overseas students because of difficulty in placing them with local firms during "sandwich" courses. Students interpreted this as a racialist measure by the college; there was a sit-in by students and some dissension among the teaching staff. The college withdrew its proposals. This is noteworthy as the only protest of importance at a college of technology; but it should be pointed out that Enfield has a particularly large department of sociology, and that it has among its academic staff a small but lively group of former LSE radicals.

UNIVERSITY OF ESSEX (SUMMER 1968)

Elsewhere the race issue was more likely to take the form of disrupting speakers, but the most significant case of a disrupted meeting concerned an entirely separate issue. Students at Essex prevented a scientist from the Government's research centre for biological warfare at Porton Down from giving a lecture at the university. (The lecture was not on the subject of germ warfare.) The incident developed into a classic disciplinary case. Dr Albert Sloman, the Vice-Chancellor of the university, and a man with a noted "liberal" reputation, sent down, without trial and purely on his own authority, three students who appeared to him to be principally involved. For Sloman this action was entirely consistent with his liberal philosophy. Freedom of speech had to be defended with exceptional rigour and sternness.

Few incidents have expressed more dramatically the gulf that exists between the old liberal and the new radical. Where Sloman saw the resolute defence of a value of free society, his student (and staff) opponents saw the arbitrary exercise of undemocratic authority. Where he saw free speech as essential to his university, they saw freedom of speech made a mockery by the fact that governments had the power to control scientists to work in the interests of developing crippling diseases.

Sloman's action was followed by (successful) demands from students for a sit-in, and a large number of members of the academic staff expressed their outrage at Sloman, either for his alleged high-handedness or for his lack of political sense. The university was virtually brought to its knees; committees were set up to consider the university's relationship with its students, and the three students were re-instated.

The usual pattern of committees to work out reforms was established, and in June proposals appeared for a reform of disciplinary measures, involving joint staff-student committees and more explicit procedures.

The left-wing groups within the student body had been very prominent during the sit-in and, as at the LSE the previous year, had succeeded in imposing their attitude on the protest as a whole. The atmosphere necessary for an emergent revolutionary leadership was there. The dispute managed to spread to issues of the complete reorganisation of the university. Because of the disruptions, there was a plea for the postponement of examinations, which rapidly became a demand for the abolition of all examinations. This tendency for demands to escalate into calls for nothing short of complete and immediate overhaul of everything is the mark of student protest at its zenith.

A free university appeared in the midst of the troubles, and initially proved far more successful than the similar attempt at the LSE, attracting up to 1,000 staff and students at its peak. However, it went into suspension for the examinations, and subsequently re-appeared as a small and desultory affair. The atmosphere necessary to its success had been dissipated. Deliberately structureless institutions can only survive while motivated by the tensions of crisis.

An important group in this Essex protest were the Situationists. These had appeared at LSE, where they enlivened the proceedings with spray-painted slogans along the school walls declaring that "Ubu cares", and by sundry acts such as releasing a flood of balloons in the course of a student meeting. The Situationists share something with other revolutionaries of modern stamp in their stress on spontaneity and the breaking free of all constraints, the refusal to accept any existing structures and modes of action – hence the balloons. But they are distinguished by their complete and determined lack of anything that can be regarded as responsibility to others; they are inveterate individualists, and thus tend to lack those rudiments of social awareness that are exhibited by most university Marxists.

At Essex they performed particular acts of courage and personal commitment during the course of the sit-in and thereby acquired a prestige that enabled them to cast their stamp on the future development of the Essex left. As a result, student revolution at Essex, although endemic, has lacked the connection with slightly more orthodox traditions of socialism that it has had at other institutions. Essex has retained a flavour of the exotic.

But the Essex germ-warfare protest had, at the time it occurred, a wider political significance. It raised the question of research into chemical and biological weapons; an issue ranging far beyond the university. Other persons not connected with the university took the opportunity to force this matter into the public eye. There was widespread debate in the mass media and attention was drawn to Porton Down in an unprecedented way. Several months later the British Government made proposals on the control of chemical weapons to the international disarmament conference in Geneva. No doubt many factors were behind this Government move; but the students of Essex can claim at least a part in the creation of public concern that led to these measures being taken.

A final element of importance at Essex was that students had for the first time in Britain* given a coherent exposition of the case that they had a right to prevent from speaking at the university those persons whom they considered to represent immoral and inhuman views or institutions. It was a paradoxical development of the Berkeley free-speech movement. One can isolate several elements in this attitude. First, there is an expression of the political frustration at working through constitutional channels which we have already discussed.

Of course, isolated acts of violence against a speaker will be as ineffective as passing a resolution in a political meeting, but their symbolic importance is that they represent a different type of action, a deliberate decision to adopt the direct, and the physical, as opposed to the constitutional and formal. The tendency towards violence in big protest marches is an important example of this development. Simply to march is to participate in the same institutionalised activity that characterised much of CND's work. To attack the police at the end of the march, to attempt (however symbolically or fruitlessly) to storm an embassy, to throw missiles, is to do something very different. The gesture says quite definitely that this is no ordinary march, subsumed as part of the political system, supervised and facilitated by the Metropolitan Police. Instead, it presages and celebrates a resort to open rebellion, ultimately to revolution.† "Today our token,

---

* It had already been done in West Germany.

† It is necessary to appreciate this point in order to understand such protests as those of opponents of *apartheid* who have damaged cricket pitches and so forth to prevent South Africans playing here. The adoption

tomorrow the real thing!" cried a leading LSE revolutionary at the close of a march to the school during the closure of February 1969.

Second, prevention of a speaker from addressing a meeting is a product of the revolutionary student's attitude to the jealously preserved freedoms of the university world. He is saying: (i) "How can you worry about such a petty value as freedom of speech when such terrible things are occurring as the Vietnam war or the manufacture of implements of chemical and biological warfare?" and (ii) "How can you be so upset about the disruption of one speech when you turn a blind eye to the vast distortion of the right to debate which is incurred by the power of capitalism in the mass media and in the control of universities?"

This latter criticism has been frequently voiced in the USA, where the autonomy of universities and their staffs is more blatantly restricted by (a) the predominance of defence contracts in university research, (b) the more detailed control of universities made possible to lay governors in the state universities, and (c) the absence of widespread security of tenure for most university teachers in contrast with Britain.

Third, hindrance of a speaker is a further challenge to the legitimacy of university authorities. It involves a group of students taking on themselves the power, usually reserved to the administration (if to anybody at all), of deciding if a person may be allowed to address an audience at the university.

These lengthy comments have been made with particular reference to the Essex incident, because that was the case where the issue was most clearly presented, but similar points apply to the several other instances of disruption that we are encountering in the course of this narrative. It may be thought that too much significance is being seen in what is

---

of self-consciously "guerrilla" tactics indicates a complete disillusion with persuasion and the political process. It is irrelevant to tell such protesters that their actions will "alienate public opinion", for that is not their concern. (January 1970).

essentially an outbreak of vandalism that differs from what occurs every week on the football terraces in little but the social status of its perpetrators. Student protest may well have provided an excuse for ideologically clothed hooliganism, but that cannot be accepted as the sole explanation. We have to show why vandalism takes the particular form it does, and why it adopts a consistent political direction. The students who participate in most student demonstrations would not, for example, be likely to join a similar effort on behalf of Mr Enoch Powell. We also have to account for the fact that many of the leaders of student revolutionary groups are far from being mindless hooligans. They are almost without exception intelligent, serious and anxious to place their actions in a philosophical context.

Although our main concern here is with student revolt in Britain, it is not possible to pass May 1968 without reference to what was occurring in France, not only for its own importance, but because it was of consequence in affecting British left-wing students in their perception of the possibilities open to them.

EVENTS OVERSEAS

A smouldering dispute at the Sorbonne had finally come to a head at the Nanterre branch of the university – which, significantly, housed the department of sociology. Although the immediate source of trouble at Nanterre had been a little dispute about student sexual behaviour,* it is clear that far more was involved. The issues ranged from dissatisfaction at the remote relationships between staff and students at the crowded French academies to the pent-up political frustration

---

* Not that the political significance of sex should be ignored. Like most quasi-religious movements, the new left attributes all its dissatisfactions to the one source – in their case the constraining restrictions imposed on man by one-dimensional capitalist society. Therefore any restraints imposed by universities on student sexual behaviour are interpreted as part of capitalism's need to prevent expressions of unrationalised spontaneity.

of nearly all forces on the left under the attenuated political life of the Fifth Republic.

This is not the place to give a full narrative of the French events, but we may note the similarity with the British situation in the ready fusion of internal university discontents with a wider political urge. British students also saw in the French events a realisation on a scale far beyond even their aspirations of widespread civil insurgency. For a brief glorious period the ultimate goal was reached, as workers in important French factories not only downed tools but occupied their factories. At one point the revolt seemed close to bringing down the republic. The token had almost become reality.

May 1968 was a month of widespread student revolt in many countries, most of which made the British protests seem very gentle and meek affairs. Several American universities were for the first time experiencing events similar to those at Berkeley. The main one was at Columbia, where a student protest against the university's decision to build student recreation facilities in open space valued by the local negro community eventually led to the occupation of the administration buildings, the raiding by students of the offices of senior members of the university, and a full expression of the student ideology of direct action, participation and rejection of the values of the surrounding society. The local society, in the form of the police force, reciprocated with a degree of violence consistent with the students' expectations.

Other American universities experiencing particularly disruptive sit-ins included Stanford, North Western and Ohio. In Germany the Free University of Berlin was again being brought to a virtual halt by recurrent student unrest. As the year progressed further German universities were the scenes of large-scale outbreaks of dissent, usually related to purely external issues – the emergency laws being passed by the Bonn Parliament and the anti-student press monopolist, Axel Springer.

In some ways the German protest movement illustrates even more clearly than the French the political position of left-wing student groups. In Germany the coalition between the conservative party (the Christian Democrats) and the party of labour (the Social Democrats) was formal, whereas in Britain its existence remained a suspicion held by those on the left. Therefore the concept of students and others forming the sole remaining basis of political opposition was more clear-cut and was formalised in the establishment of the Extra-Parliamentary Opposition (APO). Similarly, the monopolistic role of Axel Springer provided evidence for the recurrent left-wing belief that the mass media are controlled in the interests of a hegemonic class conspiracy.

In May students were also protesting in Rome (where massive and bitter confrontations took place between police, left-wing students and fascist students), Geneva, Milan, Brussels and Vienna. Students in Belgrade managed to elicit the temporary support of their Government in their demonstrations and, under somewhat different social conditions from the above, students were involved in direct political action in Madrid, Brazil, Chile, Jakarta and Tokyo. In March there had been violent clashes between students and police in Poland,* and by July students had become involved in the major political upheaval of Czechoslovakia.

Britain remained far quieter. Although theoretically all these activities have had immense importance in increasing the self-consciousness of British students, strengthening their determination to create an on-going movement and affirming their faith that this is possible, there was little immediate imitative response. At the LSE there was a desultory one-night sit-in in solidarity with the French, but other protests in England in May were more parochial.

At Oxford, where a distinguished committee† had already

* In contrast with the Czech reformers, several of the most important rebels in Poland were of a political persuasion similar to that of the British groups discussed in this book. A significant manifesto by two Polish dissidents was translated and published in Britain by International Socialism, the organisation to which the leading LSE revolutionaries belonged.

† The committee, under the chairmanship of H. L. A. Hart, professor of jurisprudence, preceded any radical activities at Oxford; in fact

been established to study the question of student representation, there was a successful attempt at removing certain
restrictions on the circulation of political leaflets by students.
Since this was one of those rules peculiar to that ancient
foundation, the incident is probably marked in revolutionary
minds as a last-ditch stand by the remnants of feudalism,
rather than a part of the capitalist class's means of suppressing free speech.

In Cambridge where, like Oxford, there had been only
minor evidence of revolutionary activity, the Vice-Chancellor, Sir Eric Ashby, established early in June a joint committee to examine a wide range of grievances. Eventually the
committee was able to propose, and see introduced, several
changes, in particular the abolition of many ancient statutes
restricting students.

A disruption of some importance at the University of Hull
gathered momentum in May and June as a radical student
carried his convictions to a rare but logical conclusion: he
refused to sit his examinations. The student concerned, Tom
Fawthrop, was the author of the tract [2] on examinations to
which reference was made in Chapter Three. For Fawthrop,
a protest against examinations was no parochial issue but
was intrinsically related to what he believed to be the whole
problem of the exploitation of man's freedom by those
authorities who seek to control his life and mould him into a
tool suited to their designs.

The sit-in that developed on Fawthrop's behalf was supported by about 200 students. No disciplinary action was

---

the protest concerning the proctorial rule about the distribution of
leaflets occurred on the day that details of the committee's establishment
were made public within the university. The inspiration behind the committee's establishment was concern at the student protest that had been
occurring elsewhere, the joint statement of the NUS and the Vice-
Chancellors, and the polite petition on representation that had been
drawn up by a wide-ranging and impeccably moderate group of students
who had made their approach through a petition to the Privy Council on
the occasion of the amendment of the university's statutes being considered by that body.[1]

taken, and the senate promised to carry out a review of the examination system; it is doubtful whether their review involved consideration of the relationship of their examinations to the exploitation of the industrial proletariat and the problem of the war in Vietnam.

THE ART COLLEGES

But during May and June the initiative had been temporarily stolen from the universities by the art colleges. Again a minor issue provided the sparking point which, after a time, enabled the development of far wider themes. Students at the Hornsey College of Art in north London started a sit-in on the issue of autonomy for their students' union and a sabbatical year for its president. But by the time the local education authority had conceded this issue some weeks later the students had dispensed with it and were enthusiastically engaged on a radical re-examination of the whole basis of art education.

As at Hull, the appearance of a fairly orthodox complaint masked a conflict extending over a vast range of issues. They had taken over the college at the start of their sit-in, and they turned it into a thoroughgoing revolutionary college. Like the LSE, Essex, Leicester and Hull before them, they came to see the protest, not simply as a blunt political weapon, but as an experience in itself which they considered valid as education, if not as a model for life in general. At the universities the idea of a free university had never really been a success; some of the plans developed at the rebel Hornsey college for the reconstruction of art education attracted the serious attention of leading figures in the sphere of art and design. It is likely that the kind of critique developed by the new left can most readily be translated into the rubric of the arts than into more academic and intellectual disciplines.

The experience of living as part of the Crouch End Commune, as they termed their occupied college, is well described by some of the participants in a book on the subject:

111

"It was in the small seminars of not more than twenty people that ideas could be thrashed out. Each person felt personally involved in the dialogue and felt the responsibility to respond vociferously to anything that was said. These discussions often went on to the small hours of the morning. If only such a situation were possible under 'normal' conditions. Never had people *en masse* participated so fully before. Never before had such energy been created within the college. People's faces were alight with excitement, as they talked more than they had ever talked before. At last we had found something that was real to all of us. We were not, after all, the complacent receivers of an inadequate educational system. We were actively concerned about our education and we wanted to participate, but we had never been given the chance before.

"What is education if it is not participation and discussion about everything which involves us? Let's hope that the people most concerned about their education do not become the victims of the educational system."[3]

The implications for "bourgeois" life in general of the model of social organisation that was being developed at Hornsey were uncannily well captured by an editorial in the *Wood Green, Southgate and Palmers Green Weekly Herald*, which is quoted in the rebels' book:

". . . a bunch of crackpots, here in Haringey, or in Grosvenor Square, or Paris, or Berlin, or Mexico, can never overthrow an established system.

"The lesson is there, staring the students in the face, although it may well take some time to penetrate through to their minds.

"They may dislike having to conform to a system in which they are required to study, and follow set programmes, and take examinations or their equivalents; and acknowledge that in doing so they are through the indulgence of others preparing themselves for a lifetime of earning, but the mere fact that they do so is not enough to alter the system.

"The system is ours. We the ordinary people, the nine-to-five, Monday-to-Friday, semi-detached, suburban wage-earners, we are the system. We are not victims of it. We are not slaves to it. We are it, and we like it.
"Does any bunch of twopenny-halfpenny kids think they can turn us upside down? They'll learn."[4]

Hornsey experienced initial hopes of success, followed by thoroughgoing failure. A committee of inquiry was established under Lord Longford, a former leader of the House of Lords. His report contained much that was in sympathy with the students' immediate demands, and was critical of the administration.

Lord Longford said that in some ways the college was run worse than any whelk-stall he knew of, and his commission proposed certain measures of student representation on an advisory academic panel. After some resistance the college authorities accepted this proposal, and the radical students appear to have been somewhat pleasantly surprised that such a commission could support them to this extent. But obviously, measures of this kind appeared essentially irrelevant to those who had experienced the participative involvement of the Crouch End Commune. The commission, however well-meaning, and the students were talking a different language.

In any case, the local authority remained in command, and used its powers enthusiastically. The local council at Haringey had passed to Conservative control in the local elections that year, and a group of mainly young and mostly inexperienced councillors controlled the borough's education services. Students and part-time staff who had been deeply implicated in the revolt were dismissed, the latter suffering the indignity of being informed of their dismissal as they arrived at the college the following November at the start of a new academic year. The re-opening had been greatly delayed by the authorities, despite opposition to such a policy by Lord Longford. Special "assessments" were carried out on students to discover whether they were "academically suitable" to be readmitted, and there was controversy surrounding the college's decision not to re-admit some of the ring-leaders of the revolt. One department, that of general studies, whose staff had been prominent in supporting the students, was decimated. First it was moved to a remote corner of the college and then it was scattered so that it no longer existed as a separate department. Finally, its part-time teachers were sent letters of dismissal without the head of the department even being informed.

Returning to May 1968, the Hornsey occupation obviously struck a chord in many art students, for very rapidly a rash of occupations started: notably at Croydon, Guildford and Birmingham. The one at Guildford reached the importance of Hornsey; the students stayed in occupation longer than did those in the North London college, far into the summer vacation, despite writs and security guards. However, at the end their numbers were greatly reduced and were in fact mainly kept going by outsiders. Surrey County Council acted with extreme sternness, dismissing students, suspending seven full-time and 35 part-time staff and changing (abolishing) many courses.* The authority refused to accept any public inquiry. The effect of all this on the morale of the remaining students and staff was severe, and the Guildford affair has continued to attract attention. In September it was announced that the seven staff and all but eight of the part-timers would be dismissed. Students at both Guildford and Hornsey staged demonstrations to protest at the delayed re-opening of their colleges. In October the National Union of Students organised a lobby of the House of Commons to support the cause of Guildford and the Association of Teachers in Technical Institutions blacklisted the college; the NUS did not do so until February 1969. In October 1969 the opening of a further academic year was greeted by a demonstration organised by the NUS and the dismissed staff and students. But Surrey County Council has been impervious to appeals.

* Just as the department of general studies suffered at Hornsey, at Guildford it was foundation studies and complementary studies.

It is an interesting comment on the difference between the sectors of education, and an unexpected one, that it should be the art students who have taken most seriously the purely educational aspects of student protest, rather than university students. A wide group of persons interested in the reform of art education established the Movement for Rethinking in Art and Design Education (MORADE).

Returning to the summer term of 1968, although this was the examination-laden end of the academic year, it continued to witness a rash of protests. At the University of Bradford there was a conflict following the dismissal of students involved in disturbances at a meeting addressed by Mr Duncan Sandys, MP.

There was also a sit-in on the issue of student representation at the University of Keele. It was demanded that student proposals be immediately accepted, but after a couple of weeks the sit-in was called off, the students resolving to work for their aims through "gentle persuasion".

An unusual incident caused trouble at the University of Leeds. Students became greatly disturbed at the activities among them of the university's security officer, and 300 students embarked on a sit-in at the end of term.

During the examinations themselves, there were occasional but not particularly serious examples of boycotts, and there was a depressing episode affecting students taking the University of London's external degree in sociology, when some examination papers were leaked before the examinations took place. Some students (not those involved in taking the examination) tried to exploit the frustrations caused by attempting, unsuccessfully, to organise a boycott of the re-sit.

SUMMARY OF DEVELOPMENTS: 1967-8

By the end of the academic year 1967–8 student protests had made an impact on the public life of the country, but it continued to be an impact out of proportion to the actual scale of events. In June it was estimated[5] that seventeen colleges and universities had become involved in some form of protest, but these were all of a trivial nature in contrast with events in other western countries. Perhaps the events assumed a greater significance in the context of Britain's usually calm political life. Further, even where the scale of events was small, people in higher education were becoming aware of the ideology which promoted them, its unfamiliarity and potential (though rarely actual) violence, and the increasing spread of its adherents.

There were also signs, greatly exaggerated in importance, of a new co-operation among dissident students at different institutions in both Britain and abroad. A Revolutionary Socialist Students Federation had been formed and had held its first conference at the LSE, being attended by prominent student activists from overseas conveniently invited to Britain by the BBC for a television programme. The Radical Students Alliance, which had tried to cover too broad a political canvas and which had become too pre-occupied with the NUS to attract the most dedicated militants, was slipping out of its never particularly important existence. The RSSF was to experience somewhat similar difficulties. Deep splits had early appeared within the main London group. It split into two factions, both claiming to be the genuine article, each accusing the other of having expropriated the funds, and each denouncing the other with at least as much venom as their several publications devoted to the capitalist class and world imperialism.

Some student protests, particularly those at Oxford, were carried out under the RSSF's banner, though there was little co-ordination. It is somewhat difficult to co-ordinate spontaneous, grass-roots activity.

But this lay in the future. In June 1968 matters appeared to be rising to a climax. The House of Lords felt moved to hold a special debate on student disorders, and the Committee of Vice-Chancellors and Principals began to consider the question of student participation. Eventually they met with the leaders of the NUS and established a common policy.

Although certain elements within the student left had early seized the concept of student power as a valid political movement, the majority of left-wing students were not so sure. The

Marxist may never depart from the position that the revolution rests with the proletariat, and relations between it and the students had not been close. Further there was a sensible reluctance by many to see students as comprising anything like a "class". But the potentialities of the student role were becoming more attractively evident, and the examples of Berlin, Paris and Columbia showed that students, if not a class, could be some kind of political force. Although most revolutionary students self-effacingly rejected Marcuse's* appeal to them to replace the proletariat as the vanguard of the revolution, they recognised that their position as students gave them certain peculiar advantages as its prophets, if not as an advance expeditionary force.

The general position of the left within the wider student body could be stated as follows at this time. The left could, in fairly small numbers, launch a disruptive protest against a political speaker that would be a self-justifying symbolic act in itself, as we have discussed above. It could also facilitate the development of an atmosphere of political tension and potential conflict that is vital to the success of an extreme-left group. If the speaker was particularly unpopular, it would also be possible to launch a large-scale protest. Such a demonstration might lead to discipline, in which case the prospects of a thorough-going sit-in were quite good.

On the issue of representation, there was evidence that, partly as the result of promptings from the National Union of Students, an increasing number of students' unions were taking up this question with determination, and a range of students extending some way beyond the Marxist left was prepared on occasions to join sit-ins and other protests on this issue. The left, although not supporting specific proposals for representation, were prepared to enter the protest and lead it in order to further their aims of fomenting a protest movement. Disciplinary issues proved somewhat similar to representation, in that they involved a challenge to the

* It is sometimes said by outside commentators that "Marcuse is the Marx of the student movement". A revolutionary student's usual reply to this is that "Marx is the Marx of the student movement".

previously accepted scope of university authority. This fact, coupled with natural feelings of identification with fellow students, made disciplinary issues a good launching point for a student protest.

MICHAELMAS TERM, 1968

The NUS planned a major campaign on student representation for the new academic year in October 1968. But the perspectives of the militants had been raised greatly beyond such mundane affairs by more developments in the USA. The police violence at the Chicago Convention of the Democratic Party had provoked a new level of tension between young American radicals and their own society. During September the town of Berkeley had been placed under a state of emergency following bitter and violent battles between police and the Berkeley left. The issues had ranged from demonstrations over the Vietnam war to resentment at the Chicago incident. In October 121 people were arrested at Berkeley following a sit-in demanding academic credit for a course on racialism given by Eldridge Cleaver.

Several universities in the USA had developed as one of their concessions to student radicalism the practice of allowing students to select certain courses for which they would be able to claim credit. The flexible American system of "course credits" makes possible such a development in a way which it would not be easy to achieve in Britain.

Obviously, most of the student-chosen courses were on race, Vietnam, urban guerrilla warfare and the like. Black students in particular, demonstrating how far American radicalism had moved from the fond hopes of a past generation of liberals, were demanding segregated courses and accommodation. The Cleaver affair marked a climax, partly because of his own criminal record and partly because the Berkeley campus was increasingly feeling the influence on its affairs of Governor Ronald Reagan.

These American developments had an impact on some English protests, but initially in the Michaelmas term British student revolt followed more characteristic paths. The group of revolutionary students at Oxford, although strong, had been unable to offer a proper protest movement of size. No doubt this is largely a result of the sprawling physical geography of the university (making a sit-in virtually impossible) and its collegiate form of organisation. However, the Oxford group was the first to start protest activities in the new academic year. When Mr Enoch Powell was due to address the Oxford Society for Individual Freedom a fierce attempt was made to prevent him. Prosecutions and fines followed in the ensuing weeks.

Later in the same month Oxford radicals protested against the matriculation ceremony. Since the theory is to be developed in the following two chapters that much of student revolt is the product of the development of the modern university, it is useful to have this reminder that much of the traditional university is also unacceptable to the new radicalism.

Enoch Powell was again, before long, the subject of a further incident—at the University of Exeter, where his meeting was abandoned after fighting had broken out. But the major event of the month was the "Vietnam weekend" at the LSE, where two elements in the student revolt received their clearest expression. First, was the fact that the university itself did not have to give offence in order to be the subject of a sit-in; and, second, it revealed the extent of deep divisions within the student body. This protest clearly bore the influence of the events in the USA. The issue was Vietnam; there were expectations (quite unfounded) of massive police violence; and most of the leaders of the LSE movement at this point were American students.

More conventional protests continued to flourish. At the University of Birmingham 100 students began a sit-in against delays over the implementation of student representation; within two months this protest was to become less conventional. At the University of Manchester 100 students sat in briefly to demand better library facilities; a rare case of a protest for limited material ends which demonstrates how once the barriers have been crossed with a particular kind of protest activity, it becomes fairly easy to organise future actions.

Much the same can be said of the rash of protests against unpopular speakers; during November these happened at the University of York (Patrick Wall) and at the Universities of Bath and Cardiff (Enoch Powell). Oxford radicals tried to force their way into a meeting of Congregation, while at the Guildford College of Art a one-day sit-in was held to protest against the re-organisation of courses which had been ordained by Surrey County Council. Influences similar to those operating at Manchester produced an abortive sit-in at the Bar, where students were becoming dissatisfied with their deplorable studying conditions.

Few of these incidents were of any importance; they would flare up and die down again. But in nearly all cases small groups of revolutionaries resembling the new left group which had grown large at the LSE could be identified. The new left was digging its still tender roots into an increasing number of universities.

Occasionally, as at the LSE, this revolutionary group was sufficiently strong to defy the majority of students. This occurred at the University of Birmingham in December, when the dispute which had started in October flared up again. There had been weeks of negotiation in a staff-student committee on the issue of representation, when the Guild of Students, obviously under the influence of a typical new-left group, escalated its demands, insisting that the committee hold its meetings in public and that a full two days of the university's academic time be devoted to mass public discussion of representation. A sit-in was started, and although at one point a mass meeting of students voted to end it, the student council decided that it should continue.

The sit-in lasted eight days, but the most significant incident was when students broke into the administrative offices, forced the Vice-Chancellor from his office and plundered confidential files. The influence of the American precedents is clear. As in the USA, some student protesters were moving away from the model of the civil rights sit-in to action informed by that of urban guerrilla warfare. They were attempting to follow the same pattern of development as that of US black militancy. A sit-in can be accommodated as a protest within a political system, in some ways appealing to other elements in that system. Physical disruption marks the end of such relationships, the surrender of hopes of achieving ends through reform, and the start of token actions of physical conflict. However appropriate this might appear in certain American contexts, it proved too much for students at Birmingham who wanted little beyond student representation. The sit-in ended without further incident, and with a new attempt at discussion and negotiation.

Another of December's events was at the usually conservative University of Bristol, where some students sought to make their embarrassingly expensive students' union building available to students from less fortunate establishments of further education elsewhere in the city. The sit-in smouldered on for some time, with increasing bitterness between different sections of the student body. The students union was against the sit-in, but the protesters were supported by large numbers of outsiders, and an attempt was made to broaden the issue far beyond that of the union building.

December also witnessed the first, and ultimately unsuccessful, attempt at introducing the "disrupted meeting" protest at the LSE, when Hugh Trevor-Roper came to deliver an oration (see Chapter Three). The first "away from home" protest by students took place when a group of Essex students tried to sit-in at the House of Commons to protest about the sale of arms to Nigeria. (The return match was played the following April, when there was a demonstration against a committee of MPs visiting the University of Essex.)

The American model of the disruptive sit-in, which had appeared briefly at Birmingham, made a further appearance, also at Essex. Following the sending down for a drugs offence of a noted Essex radical, a sit-in was started in the course of which the university's computer centre was invaded and irreparable damage caused to some research that was being programmed. American models were also followed the next day at the University of Glasgow, where 150 members of the Socialist Society protested against the opening lecture of a series on military defence in the extra-mural department. This was a protest very much in line with militant student theory, being directed against the interference of military activity in the university, and thus accusing the university of giving support to class oppression, imperialism and the like.

LENT AND SUMMER TERMS, 1969

The Michaelmas term had thus seen several major upheavals and a rash of minor incidents. The heightening tension that had built up before the summer vacation had been successfully recaptured. The disruption of meetings continued throughout the year, being mainly focused on Enoch Powell. A new cause was discovered in the Lent term with the "gates" issue at the LSE, which sparked off several little demonstrations of solidarity. These only reached the level of a sit-in at Southampton (a very minor affair) and at Cambridge, where a small group set themselves the ambitious task of dismantling all the university's gates, spikes and railings. But the weight of centuries provided a tougher resistance to the revolution than the innovations at the LSE, and the rebels managed little more than an ineffectual occupation of the Council Room.

More important matters were becoming the concern of students at Queen's University, Belfast, where the growth of a strong new-left movement was giving its distinctive flavour to Ireland's traditional concerns. Students played an important part in the subsequent eruptions of the civil rights campaign there. South of the border student unrest reached both University College and Trinity College in Dublin. At the former there was a sit-in against bureaucracy and excessive growth, and at Trinity the Minister of Education was roughly handled during a visit.

For the rest of the year there continued to be wide interest in student revolt. The Lords devoted another debate to it in April, and the Secretary of State for Education and Science,

Mr Edward Short, found occasion to condemn the revolutionaries at the LSE. But with two exceptions most of the protests from March onwards surrounded an attempt to study student unrest itself – the Select Committee on Education of the House of Commons which had been in action since November 1968 prowling around various universities and colleges.

The exceptions were the continuing saga of the LSE and a small sit-in by 70 Guildford students calling for Government action on the anniversary of their occupation. But they announced in advance that they would only sit-in for a short while, and the authorities ignored them.

Members of the Select Committee no doubt considered it to be a radical step towards democracy and participative government for a committee of the House of Commons to tour the country and visit people "at the grass roots". Among radical students it was more likely to be seen as living evidence of the growing interference in the affairs of the university by the monolith of state capitalism. So wide has the gulf between old Labourites and the new left grown that the latter may on occasions find common cause (against the former) with the conservative defenders of university privilege.

In March the Select Committee visited the University College at Swansea. Students there had called for immediate negotiations on representation. A committee had been duly established with student representation. Characteristically, the students then escalated their demand and, under the influence of the RSSF faction, produced radical proposals for the total "democratisation" of the college, including the annual election of the principal and vice-principal by all members of the college. They threatened to sit-in if no progress was made on this, and the council of the university responded somewhat strangely by unilaterally changing the role and composition of the joint committee. Matters reached a climax with the visit of the Select Committee, and a sit-in started soon afterwards. It ended after a time, but there were threats of a renewal the following year.

The Select Committee moved on to the University of Essex, where its members were subjected to constant barracking. A student swept their papers to the ground and the proceedings were reduced to a shambles. MPs left the room with students trying physically to hinder them. The clash between the new politics and the old had taken a direct form. The House of Commons referred the matter to its Committee of Privileges, but little of substance followed. Shortly afterwards the Committee went to the LSE, where its experience was somewhat similar. The year ended with the LSE affair dribbling to its close.

CONCLUSION

As in the previous year, the mass media and the revolutionaries together had successfully created an impression of virtually endemic disorder in British universities. As we have seen, the image was only partly justified. Many universities had experienced "events", but few had borne the brunt of a well-entrenched revolutionary group. Nevertheless, sufficient had occurred to make possible certain conclusions and generalisations, and further assistance in this process of analysis is provided by the growing literature of the revolutionaries, which enables us to place activities in the context of certain ideas and motivations. The following is an attempt to provide some kind of classificatory summary:

(i) The most frequent form of protest remained the disruption of meetings to be addressed by unpopular, usually political, speakers. Sometimes this appears to happen in a general feeling of outrage at such a figure as Enoch Powell, but usually there lay in the background a more developed theory of the appropriateness of such action. The rejection of "rational argument" and the resort to direct action were a deliberate rejection of both a form of political activity and a form of academic behaviour in exchange for an alternative model.

(ii) Second in importance comes a varied group of protests concerned either with the assertion of a particular student right (e.g., free speech) or a denial of certain rights to the university authority. The assertion or denial takes the form of direct action. (We are excluding here the special cases of participation in university government and disciplinary protests, which are treated separately.) Above all, these protests suggest a changed attitude among students to power and authority in the university. There was a willingness to use direct action whereas in an earlier period there would have been merely petition, solicitation and the passing of abusive resolutions. Similarly there was a growing willingness to challenge the area of operation assumed by authority and to question it, not simply in theory but in action.

(iii) Closely related to the above, and a further prominent issue in protests, has been the demand for participation in university government. There has been a growing unwillingness by students to accept as legitimate a university authority that does not include their representatives within its structure. But the demand for participation also involves something wider. It is not simply a mundane sharing in administrative decision-making that is sought, but also that meaning of participation that embraces involvement, personal satisfaction and meaningfulness. This is prominent in the critique of bureaucracy as an "impersonal" form of government.

(iv) Next in prominence have been protests concerned with different aspects of the relationship between the university and what are considered to be the forces of darkness in the outside world – the state (particularly its defence activities), industry, racialism. There may be concern at the role of lay governors in the university's affairs, and here the protest is not against lay governors as such but against the kind of interest normally represented; there may be an attempt to reveal connections between the university and certain outside agencies; there may be concern at the use of the university's resources by these outside interests, or there has been unrest at apparent interference by Government and Parliament, seen as representatives of these interests. Finally, we should also place under this heading those debates where the university is used as some kind of representative of all evil authority and made a vicarious target of protest. Although several protests can be grouped under this general heading, instances of the individual types have usually been isolated cases. This whole form of protest is of greater importance in revolutionary literature than in practical protest.*

(v) Several protests have involved resentment at university disciplinary action. This is a further case of a denial of the authorities' right to act. It also gives evidence of a willingness by students to use direct action as a countervailing force against the power of the disciplinary tribunal.

(vi) A further element in protest is the tendency of student revolts to become ends in themselves; to be used not simply to raise a protest or establish a countervailing power but to establish an alternative structure of activity, an alternative source of authoritative legitimacy, and an alternative set of values and modes of behaviour. One instance of this is the establishment of free universities as both part of a protest and a consequence of a protest. This differs somewhat from the above list of factors: they represented causes of revolt in the sense that cause can mean "irritant", provocative factor or issue. However, the element of the protest as end-in-itself may well be a "cause" in the sense of motivation.

(vii) Purely educational issues have predominated in only a few revolts, although the idea that education is in some way polluted by capitalism and the like is an important theme under (iv) above. Where education has figured directly it has concerned either course content or examinations.

(viii) Finally, while we concentrate on the critique of bureaucratic authority that emerges in a student protest, we do well to remember the small incidents at Oxford which have demonstrated the revolutionaries' contempt for the forms of the pre-bureaucratic traditional model of university authority.

Behind these different focuses of student revolt stand three major and related areas of concern. These are the questions of authority and community, and the university's relation-

* But see pp 11, 12.

ship to the outside world. Authority is an extremely important issue. It figures most prominently in the new willingness of students to resort to direct action to defy constituted authorities, in the demand for participation, in the rejection of discipline, and, if we consider academic authority as well as administrative, in the purely educational revolts. It emerges in the attack on traditional authority, and traces of it may be observed in the establishment of a counter-authority in the course of a sit-in or free university.

The elusive issue of community is seen clearly in those aspects of the demand for participation that appear to refer to personal involvement rather than to the instrumental activity of decision-making. It appears again in the structure developed by the protest as an activity in the course of a sit-in or free university, and also figures in the critique of education articulated by the new left.

Finally, concern at the relationship between the university and the world is obviously the major factor in the group of protests that we have listed under that heading. However, it is also very much involved in the disruption of political meetings that has featured so prominently in student revolt, and also in the educational critique.

It is to a further analysis of these three broad areas of concern that we now turn in successive chapters. We shall then, in Chapter Eight, bring the three areas back into relation to each other in the wider political context.

REFERENCES

1. University of Oxford, *Report of the Committee on Relations with Junior Members*, 1969, p 14 *et seq*
2. Fawthrop, T., *Education or Examination*, 1968
3. Students and Staff of Hornsey College of Art, *The Hornsey Affair*, 1969, pp 38, 39
4. *ibid*, p 207
5. *Times Educational Supplement*, June 14 1968

PART TWO

*An Analysis of
Student Revolt*

CHAPTER FIVE

Of Authority

A conflict surrounding authority is central to any student protest of importance. If we have a satisfactory model of authority in the university, its relationship to its students, and the motivations and sources of cohesion that sustain both the authority and the challenges that are made to it, we shall be in a position to understand much of what takes place during an outbreak of student unrest.

In this chapter we shall try to establish such a model, and to relate to it the issues that have emerged in the course of the contemporary student movement.*

I propose to start by differentiating four different types of authority in the university, for university authority is not homogeneous. We then consider the means by which this authority is asserted, which makes possible some prediction of the likely pattern of responses by authority to a protest. Turning our attention from the authorities to the students, we relate various strands of the movement to the different types of authority that we have identified; most of the discussion here centres on the problem of participation. Finally, from this pattern of conflict we are able to draw certain preliminary conclusions about the structure of authority that is developed within the student movement itself, and how this relates to typical constituted authority.

Universities are remarkably unlike most other large formal institutions (e.g., industries, the army, the church) in that a

---

* The scope of the model is limited to British universities. It cannot be extended without modification to either universities in other countries or other institutions of higher and further education in Britain.

wide range of autonomy and personal freedom is left to the individuals working within them, particularly the academic staff.[1] Thus there is no hard and fast hierarchy of authority through which decisions concerning the objectives of the institution and its ways of achieving them can be passed from a decision-making "top" to a merely executive "bottom". However, within this basic model of a large degree of autonomy, there are certain areas where group decisions, or decisions affecting groups of persons, will need to be made other than by the individual acting alone. This exercise of authority takes the following different forms:

(1) The delegation of decision-making power to committees of peers (cameral authority). Many decisions in university life are too complex, time-consuming and technical for everyone to be actively involved in making them. A large amount of this work will therefore be delegated to committees of fellow academics (or of fellow students in the case of students' affairs). Sometimes these committees will simply be given the task of reporting to a general meeting which has, and uses, power to change, even in details, their recommendations. However, often these committees will, either formally or in practice, have power to have their decisions implemented. In this case they can be said to possess a degree of authority.

(2) Academic authority. All universities make distinctions among their members which are intended to be based on some criteria of academic proficiency. An important division is that between staff and students, but there are also different ranks among the staff, and students may be divided as between graduate and undergraduate, honours degree and ordinary degree, degree students and diploma students. It is usual for an individual's ability to affect decision-making, at least on academic issues, to depend to a high degree on his status in this hierarchy. In this way a high degree of authority adheres to high academic rank.

(3) Administrative authority. As a fairly large community, the university needs certain tasks to be performed to facilitate

its operation. These are delegated to an administrative bureaucracy. Although in theory this is the servant of the rest of the university and exists merely to satisfy its needs, in reality it is given responsibility for the conduct of its tasks and therefore requires a degree of autonomous authority.

(4) Authority of a court of governors. Although universities are more free than most institutions from the rule "He who pays the piper . . .", they receive a vast proportion of their funds from public sources. Therefore in nearly every case the university is required to have a governing body of mainly outside persons.* In theory this governing body has many powers, but in practice they are usually delegated to committees or officers of the institution.

Finally, there is of course considerable influence exercised over universities by the Government (principally by way of the University Grants Committee) and by industrial sponsorship of research. However, except in so far as members of a university are subject as citizens to the Government's general civil authority, this influence cannot really be classed as "authority". The other external influences only become authority when mediated through one or other of the above-listed authorities.

THE ROOTS OF UNIVERSITY AUTHORITY

The next problem is to determine how authority is maintained. All the above authority types require for their effective operation certain sources of strength and sources of legitimacy. In most institutions authority rests on a combination of the accepted use of (i) coercion, (ii) habitual acceptance occasionally dignified in the form of tradition, and (iii) voluntary consent. Since the university is a voluntary association whose members have a strong personal interest in continuing to be such, the institution's greatest and ultimate sanction is that of expulsion. There are, however, strong disincentives to using this power, because of the importance of

* The major exceptions are the universities of Oxford and Cambridge.

tolerance and academic freedom in the university's code of ethics. It is therefore a weapon to which the university can have recourse only *in extremis*.

Apart from the clumsy device of temporary suspension, the only other major weapons the university authorities can wield over their members are (in the case of staff) failure in promotion or (in the case of both staff and students) giving a poor reference when employment is sought outside that particular institution. Thus the authorities in a university experience difficulties if they seek to maintain their position, or assert it under challenge, through an act of coercion. Further, coercion is usually available directly to the administrative bureaucracy and governing body alone. If academic and cameral authority seek to exercise coercion, they normally have to do so through these channels.

Voluntary, conscious consent also plays a small role in the conduct of everyday affairs. For the subject of an authority to give such consent, to go through the act of working out explicitly and rationally why authority should be respected and given legitimacy, is a rare phenomenon, even in a university. Such a questioning implies a potential challenge to that authority, for it means that the question as to why one should pay any respect to it must be raised. It is generally the case in political philosophy that arguments justifying the *status quo* are only developed after a challenge of some kind; hence the name "reactionary". For someone in a university to reach the position of voluntary, conscious consent he must be able to accept that the authority he is called upon to defend will both (a) facilitate the pursuit of goals which he shares and (b) safeguard certain values which he also shares.

Thus the main day-to-day basis of university authority is habit. Authority is obeyed because it is there; because we are accustomed, in many walks of life, to obeying such authorities; because in any case the authority makes few arduous demands on us, so that we scarcely notice it; and finally, perhaps, because it takes more effort to oppose an authority than to abide with it. In some cases, particularly in the ancient

134

universities, this habitual allegiance is made much more secure through the development of traditions.

A more widespread and related phenomenon is the attachment of high status honour to the occupants of authoritative positions. Tradition and the maintenance of status honour share with habit the absence of both the critical questioning and the subjection of an institution to rational examination according to explicit criteria which typifies voluntary consent.* But they share with conscious consent a positive awareness of the appropriateness and validity of the institution, which habit lacks. To honour something with tradition is to give it a quality akin to the sacred, the unquestionable.

Tradition can only survive within a group where the basic values that support the tradition are deeply revered and unquestioned by all concerned. Once tradition has been radically questioned it is forced to defend itself on rational grounds and ceases to be pure tradition. A factor making the hold of authorities in the university yet more tenuous is that this support of tradition is being eroded. This question of the great decline of certain features of traditionalism is crucially important to changing patterns of university authority and needs to be remarked here as a very substantial element in the background to the student challenge to university authority. However, the question extends beyond that of authority alone and is therefore discussed in fuller detail in the following chapter.

Closely related to the decline of traditional authoritative forms is the rise of bureaucratic elements in university authority. Again, the wider implications of this will be considered in Chapter Six, although we shall have occasion to refer to some of its implications at several instances in the present chapter. Not only does bureaucracy lack much of the hold on loyalty of the traditional forms; it also provides considerable scope for minor irritations and involves an element of remoteness and complexity that provides many seeds of disaffection, and much scope for protest movements.

* This is not to deny that the hierarchy may be accepted for conscious rational reasons.

CHALLENGE TO AUTHORITY

This fragile basis of university authority becomes important when the authority is challenged. The authority will be in an extremely exposed position once a significant section of the institution's membership has abandoned its habitual acceptance, applied the test of conscious consent according to the two criteria mentioned above, and judged the institution wanting. Of course, such questioning may lead to the conclusion that the authority is based on excellent grounds and should be supported.

This is unlikely to happen in the first instance because habitual modes of action will only be questioned if there are *prima facie* grounds for suspecting that the authority has become unacceptable. Thus the usual result of an examination of the basis of university authority has been rebellion against it and a demand for reform or revolution. It usually requires some action by the authority which gives offence to produce the chain of questioning; if a small agitational group simply sets out, without even provoking the authority to hasty action, to produce a critique of authority, it is unlikely that the questioning will extend beyond a very few.

If the rebellion manages to take the form of activity that the authority is not prepared to tolerate, the authority will move to take steps to fill the gap left by the withdrawal of habitual assent. Of course, an important variable at this stage will be what the authority defines for itself as intolerable. In December 1966 the administration at the LSE decided that a letter to *The Times* was sufficient to warrant disciplinary action; in 1968 and 1969 the same institution decided that unauthorised occupations of the School could be ignored.

But if authority does act it is likely to be in the direction of coercion and discipline. The establishment of conscious consent takes time, and is not available in a crisis. Thus the early stages of a university conflict may well be characterised by the disciplining and/or the expulsion of dissident elements. This has been the case at the LSE in 1966, 1967 and 1969, in Essex in 1968, Sussex and elsewhere. But this may not have the desired result. If the university community at large shares the authority's view of the "offence", as appears to have happened at Sussex, or if fear of further reprisals is sufficiently strong, the authority may escape, or even emerge strengthened. But more frequently discipline will be seen as a non-academic way of resolving disputes and may well cause considerable unrest and a further, more extensive, challenge to the authority's legitimacy. It has often been remarked how, if a university disciplines a group of not particularly popular militants, the latter rapidly become folk heroes.

University authorities are in a cleft stick; by using one of the props of their position (coercion) they are likely to sacrifice the chance of attaining another (voluntary acceptance). They are considered to be taking action that itself violates the value they are purporting to defend. The case that illustrates this dilemma most clearly is that of Dr Sloman at Essex, when his use of strong action in defence of academic freedom and free speech was itself seen to be an offence against these same values.

Thus an authority may find, once it has embarked on repression, that it must use more. Or, more likely, it will seek a non-coercive solution by going out to the membership of the institution to repair the breaches and seek that rare phenomenon, voluntary consent. This involves a process of debate and articulate defence of the grounds of authority. If the original dissatisfaction was on any considerable scale, it will also involve seeking reforms in the direction indicated by that dissatisfaction; it will be little use simply trying to rally support for the existing system. In other words, after a breakdown of habitual acceptance and the failure of coercion, there will be an offer to renegotiate the social contract in an attempt to reach a new level of equilibrium.

Thus outbreaks of student revolt are nearly always followed by a rash of staff-student committees, proposals to consider student representation, and inquiries. This happened at the LSE, where students were eventually co-opted on to the committee on the machinery of government, at Essex, Leicester, Hull, Swansea and elsewhere. Some authorities have had the advantage of the experience of their less fortunate colleagues elsewhere and have tried to move to this second stage before a serious incident of the first outbreak and reaction has occurred. This has taken place at Oxford, Reading and Cambridge. Such universities may be considered to experience the first stage of revolt vicariously.

It is interesting at this stage to contrast the position of the universities with that of the colleges of art. We are placing considerable emphasis in this analysis on the importance of the strong values of freedom and autonomy in universities, and the impossible position in which this may leave authorities who find themselves charged with the responsibility to ensure good order but denied by the norms of the institution the power with which to exercise that responsibility.

Colleges of art share neither the history and tradition of the universities, nor their concepts of autonomy and academic freedom. Like colleges of technology, they are governed by local education authorities, and their staff are regarded as employees. Thus although the Hornsey dispute saw a considerable amount of politicking and shows of compromise, it was possible for the college to dismiss some part-time members of staff at virtually no notice. Further, although the usual committee of inquiry followed the dispute, this was set up by the Department of Education and Science and not by the college authorities themselves. Similarly, at the Guildford School of Art it was possible for the Surrey County Council both to dismiss a number of staff and students, and to extinguish a range of courses considered to be those that attracted "trouble-makers". All this has not been accomplished without a good deal of protest, but the protest has been singularly ineffective. This suggests that the time-honoured doctrine of university freedom may protect militant students within the universities better than the strength of their own protest movement.

The fate of a university's attempts to seek a new basis of consent will depend very much on the issues involved, and we shall consider some of these later on. At present we are more concerned with the form than with the content of conflict. If the attempts at responding to a student challenge are successful, the institution will settle down with little disruption under its amended code, or alternatively students may simply lose interest in the whole issue. This has happened at several of the universities discussed in Chapter Four.

But it is always possible that such attempts will fail. The gap between what the authorities are able or willing to concede and what the dissidents are prepared to accept may be so vast that there can be no renegotiation. In such circumstances it is likely that the pattern of response will come full circle and there will again be resort to coercion and expulsion. One thus expects to see coercion used in the early and then in the much later stages of a prolonged conflict. So far only the LSE,* which of course started its career of student protest earliest, and possibly also Essex, have reached this depressing stage. But it is not simply a matter of just once again resorting to discipline. Everyone will be much wiser about such disputes than they were at the outset. There will have been debate about what universities should be doing, what freedoms ought to exist in them, and so forth. The authority will be uncomfortably aware of what happened during its previous attempt to take strong action. There is thus likely to be a vigorous attempt by the authority to persuade and convert the student body. This will involve drawing attention to the reforms that it is prepared to make, and also attempting to call on the support of the rest of the university in its action of discipline. The dissidents will be represented as offending the values of the institution.

We saw in Chapter Three how this had been done at the LSE as the administration attempted to achieve a new consensus based on (i) acceptance by the School of a measure of student representation and (ii) acceptance by the students that violence must be rejected as a means of resolving disputes within the university. Similarly, when disciplinary

* This refers to Britain. Several American universities have reached this position of endemic protest, while others have done so vicariously, *ie* their response to student protest has been guided by the fate of attempts at conciliation elsewhere.

action was taken against members of staff, it was based on their breach of the norm of non-violence.

It is difficult to foresee the subsequent development of a conflict after this stage, but it is likely to continue to be some continued combination of reform and coercion. Coercion here serves two purposes. It can be used, as suggested above, to restore the consensus and re-affirm its values. But it is also used *pour encourager les autres*. In an institution where dispute becomes endemic, this may well be the way in which it is finally ended. The other two available options are (a) that eventually the bulk of the students will come to regard the militants' campaigns as either undesirable or boring, leaving the university free to ignore or expel the dissidents, or (b) there will be a state of chronic dispute. One by-product of the whole exercise, besides likely reforms and changes, not only in representation but throughout the field of staff-student relations, is likely to be a decline in the liberalism of the institution.

We have seen that a more than usual degree of autonomy is granted the members of universities, but few institutions grant freedom with no reciprocal obligation. Radical students' institutions are by no means an exception here; the cost of freedom from the constraints of the outside world is a heavy ideological conformity. Similarly, the large degree of freedom in universities is predicated on the acceptance by members of certain self-imposed constraints. A devotion to learning and a tolerance of other people's values and interests are demanded. If these do not exist, if the freedoms are being pressed to their limits, there is likely to be reaction. Not only will there be internal discipline, but criteria of admission to the institution are likely to be employed to reduce the number of its members who are totally at variance with its structure and major activities.

The above analysis has been largely formal, and has concentrated on university authorities, their problems and their responses. We must now consider the substantive issues which tend to become the focus of discontent. In so doing we shall encounter more of the students' position. The challenges to authority can be related broadly to the four types or sources of authority in universities, although there is considerable overlap.

STUDENT PARTICIPATION

First, we must consider the demand by students for participation as it relates to two of the types of university authority: that of committees and that of the administrative bureaucracy. It has of course been the issue that has predominated in many disputes. It was also one of the main themes of the agreed document produced by the Committee of Vice-Chancellors and the National Union of Students, and has been the subject of several reports of university committees.

At Oxford, the Hart Committee[2] produced weighty reasons why there should be far more formal communication of university affairs to students, and also saw the need for standing joint committees of academics and students which would consider various issues and would be "armed with rights of access to parent bodies". The committee baulked, however, at the prospect of students being directly represented on governing bodies concerned with academic business, whether in large or small numbers.

The Committee on the Machinery of Government at the LSE[3] advocated direct student membership of certain decision-making bodies of the kind that Hart at Oxford was later to reject, although a large minority of members of the committee would have preferred something on the lines of Hart's "joint committees with access".

Among the many other documents on these themes that have emerged from individual universities, attention should be drawn to that produced by a staff-student working party at the University of York,[4] under the chairmanship of G. C. Moodie, professor of politics. From the outset the document recognised the conflict over authority as one of the roots of student unrest, and went on to consider increased student representation in that authority as a potential harmonious resolution.

Related to representation is the question of disciplinary authority. Discipline is in a way an instance of the demand for representation. It is easy to relate this whole series of demands to the idea of challenge to authority. Students are reaching the position where they are not prepared to ascribe legitimacy to a university authority unless they are formally represented within its decision-making structure. Partly this probably results from the changing expectations and views of their own role of the present generation of young people, for a full explanation of which one has to delve into the post-war history of increasing general affluence, the relaxation of Victorian concepts of youth's role, and the emergence of an economically important youth market. Partly, also, it relates to the changes that have taken place in universities as they have grown in size and administrative complexity.

We shall here be discussing participation in the context of power and influence, but the popularity of participation is not only used in this way. It also involves involvement, personal fulfilment and satisfaction, community. This ambiguous meaning of the word has been responsible for much of the confusion and woolly thinking on the subject. In this chapter we shall discuss participation in the sense of sharing in authority, in the following chapter we shall turn to other implications. Of course, the two are not separate. Exercising participation in the sense of wielding some form of power involves the experience of personal involvement, and implied in the notion of involvement there is often some sense of, or substitute for, the exercise of power.

For example, demands for student participation are related in some way to the decline of the traditional small college. Now, the small college did not necessarily give students any more power than the large university, although they may have felt they had more influence through face-to-face contact. Nevertheless, something of a feeling of powerlessness emerges when authority is complicated and difficult to understand, where administration is remote and operates through specialised intermediaries, where roles are specialised and formalised. This contrasts with the situation in the traditional college. Having noted the way in which the political and involvement aspects of participation are linked, we are from now on in this chapter to be concerned with the former. Thus, when we speak here of the problem of the complexity of administration, we are concerned with its implications for the student feeling difficulty in influencing it, rather than his feelings of personal isolation or alienation.

What form is a demand for participation likely to take? We can detect several possible levels, the first and most minimal of which is a demand for communication, the simple demand to know what is happening or what is about to happen. When the problem is diagnosed in this way it is concerned overwhelmingly with the argument of administrative complexity. It is ironic that this complexity of university decision-making processes, which is so often a source of irritation and feelings of remoteness by students, is in fact largely an expression of the democracy, or indeed near anarchy, of universities. As we have pointed out, a university is not a unified hierarchy. Decisions rarely pass rapidly down a chain of command. A whole range of veto groups demand a right to examine a proposal, consider it, change it or reject it. Therefore not only is it very difficult to identify a decision-making process, but issues are likely to remain within its labyrinth for a very long time.

One of the clearest exponents of more and better communications as a solution to student unrest is Bernard Crick, who has summed up the issue in the following way:

". . . I will argue that the communication network is more important than the participation network. Increasing student participation is important: but it is less important than explaining much more and much more publicly how decisions are made. If university authorities do not understand this (which I think is elementary social science) they will be puzzled when they discover that the real steps many are now taking to increase student participation and to set up more and more staff-student committees will be denounced as 'bureaucratic' by the very people they thought wanted them, and will not, of themselves, allay the present stirrings and discontents. Perhaps they should not hope for too much in any case, for many of the reasons for the present stirrings and discontents are quite beyond the control of the universities. Some of the causes are very general and we should not forget in all this discussion that in Churches, Trade Unions, Businesses, Firms, Banks, Local Government Authorities, and even in Parliament and Government Departments, people are beginning to demand greater consultation before decisions are made in their name or to bind them."[5]

If one acknowledges that several of the problems of dissent are the result of scale and sheer complexity, then improved communications may contribute to a resolution. It is only through such measures that something of the closeness of the small college can be recaptured in the large modern institution.

But by itself it may not go far enough. It assumes that the decision-making process is purely administrative and non-political. There is no question that the decisions will be influenced by interest groups, and that perhaps students constitute one such group, but one which is not as a rule in a position to apply pressure. This essentially unitary view of the university is traditionally the view of any institution taken by the group holding authority within it. One sees similar processes in industry, where it is necessary for management to have all industrial disputes regarded as failures of communications. Governments similarly diagnose disagreements between themselves and their supporters, or their national unpopularity, as the result of misunderstanding, of failure "to get the policies across".

Groups with authority can rarely admit that they have ignored or acted against certain interest groups, for their position is strengthened if it can be seen to be a consensual one in which differences of interest disappear and in which as a consequence none need feel opposed to the authorities. Despite the undoubted validity of the diagnosis of communications failure, it is unlikely that increased communications will be accepted as sufficient to fulfil student demands, no matter how "moderate" the student group concerned. Apart from its political naïvety, the communications approach smacks of a paternalism that has become distinctly unfashionable.

Proposals for improved communications are likely to be regarded as paternalistic because they tend to regard communication as one-way. Therefore a more frequent proposal by universities and others is that there should be "consultation" with students. This goes further in that it accepts that students have something to contribute to the discussion of issues, and also accepts that they have a right and ability to take part in argument and debate with those responsible for decision-making. It stops the consultation short at the point of actually sharing in power. Apart from this fact the consultation approach rests on very similar grounds as "improved communications". It may, however, be going further than simply being concerned with the complexity of decision-making. It accepts that the administrative bureaucracy and the other decision-making groups should be subject to some inquiry and pressure from students.

Academics are often extremely insistent that consultation is the proper limit of student influence. Their view rests on the concept of the university as a community of members seeking the same ends, that there are no legitimate divisions of interests between staff and students, and that some members of this community are qualified to guide its affairs while others are not equipped to do so. An interesting example of this approach is that of John Sparrow, who says (approvingly) of proposals from Oxford students for more consultation:

"The form and substance of the students' demand, therefore, suggest that it is not to seek power, but to remedy a breakdown in communications; they want to be assured that those who are on the other side of the gulf that separates, or seems to separate, the teachers from the taught, really listen to their representations, understand what they are saying, and are concerned about their interests." [6]

Academics holding such views are genuinely hurt by claims that student participation should go further. It implies a lack of faith and trust in the benevolence of the academic hierarchy and introduces an element into university life that many lecturers consider to be contrary to the very concept of a university. Again, Sparrow is a good example of this feeling:

"Representation . . . would introduce into the life of the University an element quite alien to a place of learning and more suited to an industrial enterprise, where workers' representatives bargain with the management in an atmosphere of mutual mistrust."[7]

Of course, besides the high-sounding phrases of these defences of academic life there is the less-exalted theme of a status group defending its rights and privileges against potential sharers of them for no better reason than that the holders of rights and privileges gain satisfaction from the knowledge that others are not allowed to share them. But that said, the ideal remains an attractive one. Universities are meant to be worlds of reason and intellectual objectivity, where vulgar entities like "interest" do not affect the settlement of issues. Further, since the task of universities is the acquisition of knowledge and the pursuit of excellence, it is easy for them to legitimise a non-democratic hierarchy as the form of their internal government.

In many ways the process of decision-making in a university, irrespective of the role of students, approximates to a consultative one. We have stressed already the absence of a clear-cut line of authority interfering with the actions of free men. If a committee at a university decides that certain teaching techniques are desirable, or if the staff of a department come to some conclusions as to what changes are necessary in a curriculum, these decisions will not be implemented automatically as if by *Diktat*. Whether any notice is taken of them or they are ignored will depend largely on whether particular individuals think they are worth while.

It can be seen from this that there are strong pressures within the university in favour of consultative arrangements with students. There is extreme reluctance to accede to demands for direct representation. Reasons for the opposition include the instability and transience of student membership; the difficulty of knowing what can legitimately be called a "student view"; the essentially disadvantageous position of people who have only been at university for a short time; the boring and time-consuming nature of much of the proceedings of decision-making bodies; the privacy required for discussion of certain academic issues. Some indication of the strength of academic feeling on such issues is evident from the mood of several discussions of the subject.

The Hart Report,[8] for example, drew attention to the students' lack of knowledge of teaching matters, and to their transience, which was considered to affect both the amount of expertise a student could acquire in the course of his service as a committee member and, perhaps more important, would limit his ability to bear long-term developments in mind when participating in important decisions. The committee also feared that students' lack of expertise would predispose towards systems of mandated delegates, which would ruin the university's consensual methods of decision-making.

The committee's main concern in supporting some form of student participation was the improvement of communications, and they felt that a system of joint committees would do this far more effectively than participation in decision-making bodies. Although the Machinery of Government Committee[9] at the LSE advocated direct representation in decision-making, much of the debate in that committee resulted from the resistance of many governors and academics to the idea of students sharing in decision-making, and the whole set of implications about the nature of the political process in university affairs that this invoked.

On some issues, such as the appointment of staff and the determination of curricula, universities are likely to resist very firmly indeed direct student representation. On these matters the strength of their case must rest on a bold assertion that democracy is not the only principle that requires to be satisfied. Academics have a responsibility for their individual disciplines, to ensure that these disciplines are developed with rigour and imparted to new generations of scholars in like manner. To compromise on this, it will be claimed, would be to betray the academic's calling.

On such a principle universities should stand a good chance of success in securing much student support. However, on matters where the integrity of the profession is not implicated, students are likely to insist on discussion of direct representation, and an important debate concerns whether such representation should be token or substantive. But first let us examine the rationale of the demand for representation itself in more detail.

John Sparrow, in the article quoted above, identifies the Oxbridge collegiate system as a safeguard against demands for representation, and the reason for this probably lies in the small and intimate scale of the college. The smaller an institution, the more interaction will there be among the members; and the more interaction, the more will be the shared assumptions and perspectives, and the less will be the scope for the development of self-conscious sectional interests. In a large institution these elements are likely to be lacking. And in the context of the modern university, where students often have very different assumptions and aspirations from the staff, there will be a gulf between them irrespective of size. These differences of perspective are discussed in more detail in the following chapter. For the present we are concerned with the importance of these differences for attitudes towards authority, and in particular for the reluctance among students to rely on informal or consultative methods of participation which they imply.

There is in addition a lack of trust by students in the traditional patterns of governance, and a suspicion of the motives and intentions that inform the university's actions. The élitist view of the university depends on the complete integrity and freedom from interest-group pressures of those in authority. But academics, like everyone else, are not above such pressures. They have an interest in the way the university is conducted, and that interest is not always the same as that of the students. They have a sectional interest in the distribution of financial and other resources within the college, in the distribution of their own time between research and teaching activities, in the allocation of physical space within the university's precincts.

To deny that such interests exist, and to deny that there is ever competition for the resources concerned between staff, students and other groups, is to deny facts which have become increasingly evident to many students. They see a certain hypocrisy in the behaviour of academics who throw up their hands in horror and exclaim that students are trying to introduce alien concepts of pressure and interest into the university, for they know that such pressures have been there for a good many years.

Indeed, it may even be granting the universities too much dignity to attribute these pressures and interests to the inevitable concomitants of growth and change; universities are not without their share of squalid inter-departmental politicking or inter-personal rivalries and squabbles. All this is so for the simple reason that universities are not inhabited by disembodied rational intellects as some of the eulogies of academic freedom would have one believe; they are inhabited by human beings, with ambitions, interests and desires like people in any other walk of life.

Once developments within universities gave students at least some small insight into how their institutions were governed, and once the effects of growth in higher education began to make themselves felt, it is not surprising that students' attention turned to the prospects for direct representation. It was the theme for the initial demand for participation raised at the LSE in the summer/autumn of 1966. It has become a major focus of attention for the NUS, and of parts of the statement issued by the NUS and the Committee of Vice-Chancellors. And as we saw in Chapter Four, it has been a leading issue in many university protests.

The rationale for these demands[10] is that it is only if students are enabled to take this direct share in university government that the atmosphere of trust, identification as members of the institution, and harmonious staff-student relationships can be restored. It is little use simply bemoaning the passing of the acquiescent students of a past generation if the environment within and outside the universities has changed. Universities will have to change if they are to conserve those aspects of their traditions that they hold most dear. If, through changes in representation and so forth, something of the integrated community of the traditional institution can be recovered, this will have been achieved. If, on the other hand, change is resisted, not only will there be no improvement in matters, but students are likely to lose interest and faith in plans for representation and move on to more militant ideas, as will be considered below.

This will not occur simply because of the impatience and instability of youth, although that is doubtless a factor. A more serious reason is that the demand for representation is essentially a moderate one; it accepts the existing framework of government and simply requests inclusion within it. If this proposal meets with rejection, there is likely to be an increase in hostility and suspicion towards the existing authorities, and disillusion with more or less restrained means of protest. We shall shortly consider how this develops, but first we must pay some attention to the difference between token and substantive representation.

Once universities have conceded the concept of representation in theory, they are likely to stake their position in defence of the merits of token membership. This enables students to know, through their representatives, exactly what is happening on various issues, and it makes it possible for students to argue their case up to and including the stage of decision-taking. It also gives students a symbolic representative status. Academics are able to concede all this without surrendering their insistence on the lack of interest-groups and other necessary frictions; this is possible because they can insist that such representatives serve as "individuals" and not, in fact, as representatives. They can also give as their reason for accepting student representatives their desire to tap a new source of ideas and views, rather than the need, in the face of student unrest, to accede to a political demand.

Sometimes, as at Leicester, student proposals for representation have not gone beyond this level, but more often it has failed to satisfy. There is fear among students that a small scale of membership will provide no effective voice, that there will be an appearance of participation but a lack of its substance, that student members will continually be outvoted, that the demand for full participation in decision-making structure is not at all met by inserting the occasional individual into a place on a committee. One solution to the problem that is likely to be tried is to seek membership on a larger scale. In this way the debate becomes one of scale of membership, and the argument is in terms of numbers. Students may here simply be seeking more members in order to increase the effectiveness of their spokesmen, or, somewhat differently, they may seek some notion of parity with the academic staff. This last is likely to be the most controversial of the proposals, and is likely to be resisted on all committees dealing with matters of major academic or administrative importance.

Various combinations of the above forms of participation are likely to be the basic ingredients of an attempt to reach agreement after an outbreak of student unrest. They represent an attempt to counter the problems incurred by the growing role of administrative bureaucracy, the growing complexity of committee structures, and the remoteness from students that these developments entail. In so far as the proposals go beyond communication and elementary consultation, they are a response to an increasing self-awareness among students as an interest in a position to impose pressure and make a contribution to the university. However, where there is an active militant left-wing group deeply involved in the protest (and this is usually the case), at least one section of the student body is unlikely to be satisfied with such a frame of reference. This will be so even where, as at the LSE and at Leicester, the far left gave initial support to such proposals in order to have an issue on which to unite students in some form of protest.

We must remember that these groups are in general

disillusioned with representative politics and are seeking new ways of exercising power on a detested political system through the use of direct action. They are also likely to entertain some form of conspiracy theory which says that the university will, by definition, act against student interests because of an on-going major conflict. Therefore, if the university is refusing student demands for representation, it is considered by the left to be a demand worth supporting. If, however, the authorities offer representation, it must be because they have worked it out to be in their own interests, and therefore revolutionary students will oppose such proposals.

This is the inevitable result of a political philosophy that excludes *a priori* the possibility of reform within the existing structures. Finally, the student left believes, as we have encountered elsewhere, that authority is continuous and monolithic. It follows from this with impeccable logic that little can really be done to improve staff-student relations in one university without an international social and cultural revolution on behalf of the world's oppressed. In the meantime, local conflicts can be engineered, partly to provide the opening shots of the revolution, partly to gain local and usually negative victories, but mainly to recruit new members to revolutionary groups and sustain the spirits of the existing membership. In this context to campaign for the representation of the student interest in the existing pattern of university decision-making is obviously written off as a dangerous diversion.

In so far as participation is concerned with gaining a share in decision-making structures, the approach to it that emerges from the revolutionaries' perspective is that students should not entangle themselves in the administrative machine and lend legitimacy to it. They should maintain their independence, and their strength, by raising demands to which it is known the university cannot accede, but which will raise student expectations. They should also organise from time to time occupations and other displays of direct action which will keep the movement going and, almost as a by-product, achieve some local objectives.

If one turns to the student movement elsewhere, this element is so obvious that it does not require separate comment; these student movements rarely bother to turn their attention to internal issues. But in Britain student revolt is often seen as resulting entirely from troubles within universities. As we are trying to demonstrate at several points in this book, this is only partly the truth. Internal problems have played their part, but their main contribution has been to parallel the external political changes against which the protest is really directed. This has become more clear at the two major locations of student revolt in Britain, the LSE and the University of Essex. In the case of the LSE, we have studied the process at length in Chapters Two and Three; and in Chapter Four we have looked briefly at the Essex protests; only rarely have they concerned the internal conditions of the University of Essex. Similar points can be illustrated from the literature of the far left: it is, for example, one of the major points to emerge from Gareth Stedman-Jones's valuable exegesis of the meaning of student revolt. He ends his essay with:

"The student movement in Britain today will only grow if it constantly and dynamically unites the struggle on the campus to the struggle against capitalist society at large. It will not ultimately succeed in achieving any substantial advances unless it wins its place within a revolutionary bloc much vaster than itself, under the hegemony of the working class. But it can meanwhile use its opportunities to act as a starting-gun for wider social conflict. The slogan of Berlin resounds through Europe: 'Today the Students – Tomorrow the Workers'."[11]

Joseph Newman similarly ascribes a global significance to the aims of student revolt:

"students . . . have played an exemplary and detonating role far beyond the confines of universities, revealing *through their own struggle* the repressive and rigid structures of domination which characterise 'Western Democracy'

and pointing towards new revolutionary modes of struggle, objectives and forms of organisation . . . .
"Student action has tended to be *reactive* to external stimuli, whereas only on the basis of mass mobilisation arising from the students' situation and the *specific* ways in which they experience societal contradictions, can the movement take root and gather momentum, making possible *initiatory* tactics and strategy, opening up fissures and revealing contradictions, overcoming the limits of corporatism through the continuous escalation of goals which are not therefore fixed in terms of any single issue or demand, laid down in advance on an *a prioristic* basis."[12]

It is probably when this stage in the development of a student protest has been reached that the university has passed, unsuccessfully, the point where there is a search for internal reforms that can be introduced with mutual agreement to restore the consensus. Some factors may limit the importance of this. First, the revolutionary group may be too small to raise any event of major significance. Second, students may adopt the position that they would prefer direct action to representation, but use it only occasionally, enabling the university to function most of the time without crisis. Third, an institution may follow the path suggested by some of the old academic left, which is never to confront the far left, to compromise where necessary, to ignore all provocation, never to take disciplinary action, even if the stage is reached where academic work is disrupted and lectures broken up.

However, if none of these escapes are taken, the university is faced with a section of its student body which no longer seeks to reform or improve the university, but which seeks to use the institution as a base for the creation of its own movement; confrontations with the authority are then used merely as exercises or recruiting sessions for the movement.

A proposal for university government that has originated on the far left is that for government by general assembly. Unless this is put forward as one of those impossible demands designed simply to rally support and provoke rather than to

154

seek change, it would seem to follow from certain important themes in the new left's thinking. The essence of the proposal is that all decisions of importance should be taken by a full meeting of the entire membership of the university – students, teachers, cleaners, porters, administrators and cooks. They would all have equal rights in decision-making, including decisions on the curriculum and the appointment of academic staff. Among the ideas that inform such a proposal one can identify the following. First, there is the deep suspicion of representatives, or even of delegates, that is characteristic of the new left. It is closely related to their general political view, which is to reject all ideas of MP's, councillors, trade union officers, and anyone else who will enter a political situation and exercise his own judgment to secure compromises and agreements without the continuous and explicit veto of the mass over his actions. Direct participation, for the left, has to be both universal and continuous. Second, there is an attempt to achieve complete equality of participation, which involves ceasing to recognise any degrees of competence. This is a subject which will be considered further when we examine challenges to the academic authority. Third, there is the ideal of the participating community, which we shall consider more fully in Chapter Six.

Finally, and more simply, the proposal is based on the kind of environment in which the student left itself flourishes: the mass meeting. Different styles of debate and argument suit different contexts. The traditional orator performs best in grand formal surroundings. The academic is likely to prefer the informal seriousness of the seminar room. The exponent of the emotive politics of direct action thrives in the mass revolutionary meeting. This too will be taken up further at later points of the discussion, in this chapter and others. It has wide implications for a study of the new left and its relation to existing patterns of political activity.

STUDENTS AND ACADEMIC AUTHORITY

We must now consider a further type of authority in universities and its relationship to student challenge: academic authority. This raises different issues from the administrative and cameral authorities with which we have been concerned in the above. Academic authority is based on neither control of resources, nor ability to use coercion, nor yet democratic election. It rests on a general acceptance of competence.

As far as the student is concerned, academic authority involves decisions as to what comprises the content and structure of courses and the form of examinations. Very few protests in this country have been explicitly concerned with academic questions. An exception was the boycott of examinations at the University of Hull, and the phenomenon noted at several universities where free universities were established as part of the aftermath of protest. And in these cases the educational protest was cast in a far broader political mould. Matters have been taken further in the USA, where students have demanded, often with success, the right to invite from outside persons who will give special courses, which count as part of the regular curriculum.

Interestingly, the only places in Britain where protest has been centrally concerned with educational content have been the colleges of art. Here the criticism seems to have spanned the board from academic dissatisfaction with educational quality to a critique which is more obviously rooted in the concerns of the new left. Discussing the way in which the students at Hornsey sought changes in their immediate environment of education, which might at first sight appear a short-sighted, non-revolutionary policy, the book produced by the Hornsey rebels says:

"But in part [this] corresponded to revolutionary necessity. Profound changes in one's immediate environment may be unrealisable without the wider revolution. However, it is no less true today – in Western conditions – that the wider revolution is unrealisable without the hope of these immediate changes, without the vivid conviction of a mutation at the very roots of living. The revolutionising of day-to-day being cannot wait on the first Five-Year Plan, the right decisions from above at the earliest possible, reasonable opportunity. Not any longer, not in our time."[13]

But if educational content has not been a predominant theme of protest, it has been an important subsidiary one. We shall see in the following chapter how certain educational matters are of relevance to student dissatisfactions, and in Chapter Seven we shall concern ourselves directly with a major element of the new left's educational critique: that of the university's entanglement in the world of government, industry and commerce. But this debate about the relationship between academic institutions and the outside world does not, by itself, necessarily undermine the concept of academic authority; it simply rejects as unworthy those elements of academic authority which are felt to have compromised their profession. The academic is seen as having sold his birthright of free intelligence for an industrial research contract. Posed thus, the criticism is far from being an attack on the notion of academic authority as such: it may even be considered a fundamental defence of it. However, individual academic authorities may be delegitimised as a result of their alleged prostitution. More radical is the challenge to the very notions of acquired knowledge and intellectual competence which has come from certain groups, mainly on the anarchistic fringe and from the USA, but with definite overtones of the Marxist theory of knowledge.

The new left have taken from the early works of Marx the message that the total structure of our social world is biased and corrupted by the class system to the extent that nearly every aspect of existing society is engaged in distorting, crushing and oppressing the human spirit. As a result this spirit is in a state of complete alienation from its true, free nature. Thus the elusive concept of species life is defined negatively as the elimination of all influences of society and environment.

(More accurately, it involves the elimination of all influences apart from those that would exist in a hypothetical post-revolutionary society; but since the content of that society is specified in no closer detail than as that society which would result if men were liberated from the influences of existing society and environment, it amounts to much the same thing.)

This philosophy of course gains much strength from the very real problems of alienation resulting from technological complexity and wage labour; these themes and their relationship to student revolt will be taken up in Chapter Eight. But the new left's analysis of alienation does not end here. Marx used the factory conditions of mid-Victorian England as the material point of reference for his conception of the totality of life in the 19th century industrial society; similarly the new left have given universal significance to the model of man in mass-production industry. All actions are seen as participating in the ordered production line ordained by capitalism, to the mental and physical detriment of the participants and to the greater glory and enrichment of the rulers.

Thus "bourgeois" knowledge, that knowledge which is taught in our universities, is seen as being but part of this system and of little or no validity save in its role in the maintenance of the existing social structure. The university is seen as part of the production line turning out management personnel to specifications demanded by international capitalism. It should, of course, be remembered that the analogy was first applied by none other than Clarke Kerr,[14] former president of Berkeley. Quotations from his writings are to be found in nearly all writings on this theme by the new left.

The "production line" imagery haunts the writing of the new left. The Hornsey students assert that "it is patently ridiculous to think that an education in innovation can be carried out in a factory atmosphere where students are conceived of as passive objects being processed along the lines of the system".[15] Blackburn and Anderson[16] have made an attempt to relate nearly all branches of study in the social sciences in Britain and elsewhere to the maintenance of an ideology supportive of class oppression and exploitation. Finally, a pamphlet produced by the International Socialists makes the point most vividly:

"A whole section of students is bewildered to find that what awaits them at the end of a long and arduous climb is not the kingdom of the mind they were promised . . . but participation in or apologetics for the world of money and militarism, poverty and police forces. Instead of being offered a chance to understand the world and society they themselves are subjected to a crude quantification; in place of an exploration of reality they get exams."[17]

This philosophy results from a combination of an extreme of the conspiracy theory and a full appreciation of the important lesson of sociology that ultimately all our knowledge is rooted in our social experience and that there is no court of appeal beyond the human situation. For the soul in search of moral and epistomological certainty, this is a discomforting experience. The only certainty is that we are very much alone in the dark, in the last analysis not even able to place complete confidence in our sense experience and having as our only source of guidance and knowledge the conflicting claims to wisdom of fellow humans who are similarly lost.

To the sensitive and intelligent young person with a leaning towards conspiracy theory, this realisation of the vulnerability of the human condition can come as a great blow; and for the modern youth it is one against which the traditional refuge of religious faith can provide no escape. Knowledge is not only socially rooted, it is also a product of a social structure that is biased and manipulated. It is here that Marxism provides a way out. With one sweep Marx's early writings take to their ultimate and terrifying conclusion all fears about the insecurity and distortion of human knowledge, and then suddenly erect in their place a new certainty, a new faith, a new conviction.

The experience is essentially a religious one. Beside it, and the celebration of it in the activities of revolutionary groups, the insistence of academics on the value of academic freedom as traditionally conceived pales into insignificance. So does all claim to superior knowledge and rational argument.[18] If all society, all knowledge, is hopelessly distorted by class bias, then ideas of rationality and the traditional appeals of liberalism for tolerance for the views of those with whom one disagrees lose all meaning. If society is hopelessly structured against the human spirit, nothing can be achieved by argument. If all views apart from that of the philosophy of total alienation are hostile to freedom, the holders of them have no moral right to speak or be heard.

Further, if all knowledge gained from existing society is biased, it follows that there can be no such thing as pure expertise or specialisation. Indeed, if the experience and knowledge one has gained are those of this twisted world, then it would be better to be entirely ignorant. In this most recent manifestation of the noble savage in political philosophy, the familiar argument that youth's "freshness of approach" sometimes gives it a unique ability is taken to its ultimate conclusion: the less one knows about a subject the more entitled one is to speak on it, because the less distorted is one's perception. Hence the general assembly of staff, students and workers. Hence student power as opposed to student representation. Since all is biased, political and subjective, very little value is placed either on factual empirical knowledge or on rigorous rational thought. The great claims to academic authority are stripped bare of their sanctity and, with the accumulation of traditions that surrounds them, thrown aside. Like all who pretend at total revolution, there is an overwhelming emphasis on the need for total renewal, total rebirth.

THE "OUTSIDERS"

Finally, a student protest may make its challenge to authority by its attack on the alleged political nature of the Court of Governors and the relationship between university, government and industry which they symbolise. Although this question has figured in several student protests, and is indeed a major background theme of the far left, it has rarely been the main-spring. The role of external governors and their authority is important for two reasons. First, left-wing students may resent the presence of such a group, and accredit no legitimacy to a group of men who appear to them to represent the interests of capitalism rather than those of learning. Thus we have seen how at the LSE authority was at its weakest when it took the form of the court of governors. Second, we must remember that the situation within a university once some kind of protest has been launched is one where the authority is in part appealing to the mass of staff and students to support it. This means making a conscious effort to demonstrate that the authority exists to further certain shared values. These values will include the need for academic work to be pursued without the interference of political bias for it is one of the far left's objectives to politicise the university. The credibility of such a claim is diminished if courts of governors are seen to be an active element of that authority.

Since our attention in this chapter has been focused on the different forms taken by authority in the university and on student response to them, it is necessary to include reference to this role of lay authority. But this question, and the closely related one of the intrusion of government and industry, deserve consideration in their own right; such is their importance, not only in student protest, but in the future development of universities. This discussion is pursued in Chapter Seven.

CONCLUSION: REVOLUTIONARY AUTHORITY

We have seen in this chapter how much of the conflict within universities can be related to discontent with various aspects of authority. It is possible to indicate individual frustrations and problems which cause unrest on a wide scale, but it is also possible to detect throughout the discussion the special place occupied by the far-left groups. These groups are not seeking feasible reform of the universities because, quite simply, they do not believe that that which is possible is worth while, or that which would be worth while is possible. Their dissatisfaction touches such fundamental problems that it is not amenable to reform. The conflict concerns the whole structure of organisation.

The following table attempts to list certain major elements

161

in the model of authority characteristic of authority in the contemporary British university, and to set against these the counter-model that appears to be developed in the writings of the new left and in their own institutional practices within a student protest.

ASPECT OF ORGANISATION	CONVENTIONAL UNIVERSITY	REVOLUTIONARY CONCEPT
Structure of roles	(in admin. structure) Seen as formal and hierarchical; roles as only a part of life	Rejection of all formal structuring. Authority lies in capturing the mood of the moment; roles are total and envelop the whole personality
Role of rules in co-ordinating authority	(in admin. structure) Authority created by and restrained by system of rules	Emergent leaders subject to no restraints other than what the movement will allow at any moment. Breach of authority's rules and unwillingness to accept restraints is a major claim for attention
Role of values	(in admin. structure) Adherence to second-order principles, formal rules and procedures	Desire to grapple continuously with the absolute and assert ultimate morality
Typical issues of discussion	(cameral authority) Problems are technical, points of detail	Everything is political and concerns clash of values and interests
Concept of academic authority	Appeal to competence within a subject; erudition and achievement	Inseparableness of value choices. Stress on immediacy of direct experience unmediated by learning formal concepts
Attitude to knowledge	(Academic authority) Scepticism; appeal to rational model of dialogue	Pursuit of certainty; commitment and belief; rejection of rational frameworks as externally imposed restraints. Emotional style
Attitude to change	Reformist	Total revolution
Central objective of authority	To maintain an on-going academic institution	To create a thorough-going revolutionary movement and/or incidents valid for their own sake as experiences

At this stage it becomes valuable to bring to bear on our data the classical sociological writing on authority structures. Elements of the Weberian[19] pattern of traditional and of legal-rational (bureaucratic) forms of authority have already figured in our discussion. We have been able to identify a decline in the hold of traditional patterns of allegiance and legitimacy, and accompanying it a rise in bureaucratic structures, with their attendant problems. The elements of university authority set out in our table correspond to a degree with the concept of a rational bureaucracy. There are important exceptions in that cameral authority is not really bureaucratic, although it is rational; further, academic authority has essentially a legitimation of its own, though as it appears in the university it is reinforced by a degree of rational justification and in some cases a traditional aura.

The student revolutionaries' pattern of counter-authority contrasts with and conflicts with the rational-bureaucratic-academic model on every count, but it can hardly be considered to represent the normal pole of rationality, that of tradition. An answer is to be found in Weber's [20] third concept of an authority type – the much-abused idea of charisma. The concept has been abused because it is loosely associated with theories of the role of "great men", and can therefore be made to appear a simplistic and not very useful theory of social change or, in different hands, it can be used to link Christ, Napoleon, Hitler and Fidel Castro in one big pejorative lump. The new left become very angry at this latter technique.[21]

But the concept refers to much more than all this. It is related to the problem of personal meaninglessness and ethical vacuum that Weber considered to be a likely concomitant of heavy bureaucratisation; in other words, it is seen as an attempt to overcome alienation. In the charismatic situation,[22] individuals attempt to break through the confining structures of an over-determined social world, to contradict the prevailing moral and social constraints and to establish radically new counters to them.

There is at the same time a frustration with the apparent

163

ethical meaninglessness behind the routinised forms of bureaucratic systems, even a desire for mystery. Charismatic activity implies a search for moral absolutes, and an insistence on the assertion of these absolutes at every instant. There may also be an attempt to transcend the normal restraints imposed on inter-personal relations by the de-emphasis on the emotional that a rationalised mode of action implies. It is part of this whole process that the leader (or leadership group) emerges as the person who is able to give expression to all these feelings and to provide the basis of certainty that the search for the charismatic craves. It is a craving for certainty that does not seek satisfaction in rational explanation nor in an appeal to an ancient authority. It is difficult in such circumstances for the source of certainty to be found in anything other than an individual or a group of men. It is in this way that "great men" are part of the charismatic, but this does not mean that the scope of the concept of charisma is limited to the idea of the "great man". The charismatic response is a response to a certain type of social situation.

This is a theme to which we shall return in Chapters Six and Eight. It should be clear by now that we are relating the concept of charisma to the model of the revolutionary counter-university set out in the table. Essentially this is a counter to a bureaucratic model, but we have also been able to suggest certain charismatic alternatives to academic and simply rational modes. Our main contention is thus that the various challenges to university authority which are made by the new left should not be seen as isolated acts of indiscipline and anarchy, nor even as the direct products of a precise ideology. They are the expression of a search for an alternative style of authority, for the fulfilment of certain demands which are made on the institutions with which the people concerned are associated. This search takes the form of the charismatic.

It is characteristic of both the new left and their enemies to describe the student revolt as being against authority, against discipline. This is not the case. The student movement seeks ethical absoluteness; it seeks certainty and belief.

It seeks a co-ordinated pattern of world revolution. It seeks an orthodoxy of revolutionary doctrine. The revolt against authority is against certain types of authority, but it is in favour of a certain other type.

It may be argued that there is an absence of great figures within the student movement, and that great figures although not the sole phenomenon in charisma, are crucial to it. This is true. However, it is entirely possible for the charisma to be maintained by a group rather than a single person, and I would suggest that the circumstances of the modern, middle-class young person (such as student revolutionaries are) pre-dispose against individuals establishing themselves as leaders, but a small group will be able to play such a role. Such groups can be found to emerge wherever student revolt exists on any scale. They do not describe themselves as a leadership, but are prepared to be regarded as a vanguard, which is sufficient.

Finally it may be objected that even if students may in some way crave the authority of secure belief and a disciplined revolution they are in practice disorganised and incapable of doing anything that is sustained and co-ordinated (rather than spasmodic and transient) without developing at least the rudiments of a conventional organisation. But this is a characteristic that always accompanies the appearance of the charismatic; its fundamental problem is its transience and its instability.

REFERENCES

1. For a useful discussion of similar questions, see Eustace, R., "The Government of Scholars" (in Martin, D. (ed), *Anarchy and Culture*, 1969)
2. University of Oxford, Report of Committee on Relations with Junior Members, 1969, p 83 *et seq*
3. London School of Economics and Political Science, Report of Committee on the Machinery of Government (Majority Report), 1968, Section H

4. University of York, *The Role of Students in the Government of the University*, 1968
5. Crick, B., "The Proper Limits of Student Influence" (in Martin, *op cit*, p 157)
6. Sparrow, J., "Revolting Students?" (in *ibid*, p 179, and in *The Listener*, July 4 1968)
7. *ibid*, p 180
8. University of Oxford, *op cit*, p 89 *et seq*
9. LSE, *op cit*, pp 14, 15
10. A succinct statement of some of the main arguments for representation can be found in Straw, J., "Participation in Practice" (in Crouch, C. (ed), *Students Today*, Fabian Society, 1968)
11. Stedman-Jones, G., "The Meaning of the Student Revolt" (in Cockburn, C. and Blackburn, R. (eds), *Student Power*, 1969, p 54)
12. Newman, J., "Education and Politics in Britain" (in Nagel, J. (ed), *Student Power*, 1969, p 14)
13. Students and Staff of the Hornsey College of Art, *The Hornsey Affair*, 1969, p 108
14. Kerr, C., *The Uses of the University*, 1963
15. Students . . . Hornsey, *op cit*, p 127
16. Blackburn, R. and Anderson, P., "The Repressive Culture" (in Cockburn and Blackburn, *op cit*)
17. Harman, C. *et alii*, Education, Capitalism and the Student Revolt (International Socialism), 1968, p 50
18. An excellent study of the relationship between disillusion with rationalism and the resurgence of a kind of religious fervour is to be found in Labedz, L., "Students and Revolution" (*Survey*, July 1968). Further articles on the theme appeared in the following issue (October 1968)
19. Weber, M., "The Types of Authority and Imperative Coordination" (in his *Theory of Social and Economic Organisation*, trans. Henderson, A. M. and Parsons, T., 1949)
20. *ibid*, p 358 *et seq*
21. see Blackburn, R., *op cit*, p 179, *et seq*
22. Eisenstadt, S. N., *Max Weber on Charisma and Institution Building*, 1968, introduction

CHAPTER SIX

Of Community and Involvement

To develop further the themes of traditionalism, bureaucracy and charisma, we need to go beyond the question of authority. It is necessary to consider the wider structures of social relationships that are characteristic of different types of institution and of which the system of authority is but a part, albeit the most important. We shall examine these three models of institutional characteristics in so far as they apply to the university; place into this framework the patterns of change that are now affecting the university; and then seek to further our understanding of the student movement as a social phenomenon within this context.

In this task we become concerned with what we have called the second aspect of participation; that of involvement and meaningfulness as opposed to instrumental decision-making. In the literature of the student left this aspect of their demand often takes the form of a demand for "community". We shall have occasion later to quarrel with the use of this term in this context, but since it has been thus used so often, we shall continue to use it until we reach a more satisfactory formulation.

The polarisation between bureaucracy and community has been a prominent one in much sociological thinking. In particular it stands behind the dichotomy between *Gemeinschaft* and *Gesellschaft* elaborated by Ferdinand Toennies.[1] How well do these models of relationships apply to changes within the university? How valid is the generalisation that academic communities are becoming bureaucratic multiversities? How do student demands for participation and radical doctrines of alienation and community involvement fit into this framework of analysis?

THE TRADITIONAL IDEAL

Important in affecting the web of relationships within a university will be the structure of authority, the presuppositions of the members and the constraints and guides imposed on the internal structure by the impingement of the outside world. On all three criteria one can allocate a fair degree of substance to the claim that the traditional university represented an "academic community". The institution was small, the essential unit being the college. A deep mould of tradition enclosed customs and practices, legitimising the hierarchy of power and status and providing a structure for relationships.

In the earliest days members were expected to remain celibate, and throughout the emergence from the Middle Ages there survived a strong tradition of commensality and of residence on the premises of the college. Everyone was thus a "member" of the college (at Oxford students are still called "junior members") although this common membership did not imply equality; it implied that such distinctions of status that existed were meet and just and ordained by a tradition which in turn moderated their operation. The traditional college thus consisted of a small, face-to-face group, self-conscious of the weight of tradition and sharing residence and common board.

There was similarly a homogeneity imparted by the presuppositions of the members. They came from a narrow social stratum, each underwent a lengthy socialisation process before gaining admittance to the community. For many centuries a strong religious consensus was demanded.

Finally, the impingement of the outside world did little to unsettle this model. This does not mean that universities were allowed to grow up in complete isolation from the outside world; indeed it is rarely realised by critics of the current trend towards vocationalism in education that the medieval university was very much a vocational institution, preparing for careers in medicine, law and, chiefly, the church. Nor should it be assumed that the university existed in quiet harmony with the surrounding world. The histories of the universities of Oxford and of Paris reveal a good deal of conflict between academy and state and between town and gown. But at its height and at its best (and it was often at the depths and its worst) the medieval university was able to establish a tradition of quietude, of reasonable isolation and autonomy, of the settled pursuit of scholarship and enjoyment of privilege.

It is from this tradition that the idea of an academic community takes its meaning, even though, as we shall see, it is not always exactly what people have in mind when they call for such a community or rush to its defence. But even when such an image is accepted certain exceptions in the university from the ideal type of community or *Gemeinschaft* need to be noted. The pursuit of knowledge will never lend itself to quite the network of unquestioning adherence to tradition that typifies the complete community. Even though the cultivation of scholarship involves a far stronger regard for tradition than does the carrying out of research, there must be at least an element of independence of mind, of questioning and innovation.

Similarly, alongside the idea of the academic community there eventually grew up the idea of academic freedom, which entails an element of independent spirit for the individual member that is not consistent with a community relationship of the strength of, say, a village. The academic community has therefore had to develop, particularly as it approached the modern period with its growing multiplicity of disciplines and philosophies, as a community of reserve; a community whose stability was not ensured simply by the strong adherence to a set of common norms but also by a respect of others' independence, a tolerance of diversity on the condition that this diversity was rooted in a fundamental consensus and did not trespass on one's own particular pursuits and interests. In other words, the university has become a community of professionals, and the professional is the last man to be found in a thorough-going community. This was a potential source of tension.

Further elements of the idealised traditional university will be revealed as we discuss it in contrast to the idealised multi-varsity.

THE IDEAL MULTI-VARSITY

The institution here is large and, perhaps more important, growing. Because of this size a large professional bureaucracy has to be developed. Whereas the "head" of a traditional college was one of the teaching body, the head of a modern university is likely to be a full-time administrator, even if for the sake of maintaining a link with the old tradition he is frequently considered a member of the academic staff. Under him is a network of full-time officers who relate to each other, the students and the teachers through formalised and special-ised bureaucratic roles.

Because the institution is either new, or undergoing rapid growth, or in the process of change and development in its departmental structure, tradition is much diminished. The trappings of tradition may well be there; most of the new foundations in Britain have tried to acquire the gowns, cere-monies and high tables of Oxford and Cambridge. But such practices will have no deep significance within the life of the college, will not represent the main orientation of its activi-ties, and will often appear *outré* or absurd.

Similarly, the characteristic pursuit of knowledge will be different. Departments of history and classics will continue to cultivate scholarship, but in the physical sciences, eco-nomics and some other of the social sciences, the major activity is research: a striving for new knowledge rejecting old concepts. Whereas the pursuit of scholarship renewed each year the common core of culture of the university's members, research is increasingly undertaken by small specialised re-search units, often having a tangential relationship with other areas of the college. Further, the specialisation of disciples, and the increasing inaccessibility of their concepts to followers of other disciplines, render communication among different faculties less possible, and the idea of a common core of culture less applicable.

Again, the forms survive. Public lectures and orations are still given by eminent professors; but what can usefully be conveyed to the assembled academic community by a one-hour oration on a specialised modern discipline?

Next, the presuppositions of the members have changed. University education is seen increasingly as "career preparation"; and modern career preparation is far removed from the generalised infusion of culture which prepared the medieval student for his later vocation. There is thus far less prior commitment to the values of the institution by a prospective member. Even in the case of a new lecturer, it is unlikely that there will be either the time or the inclination to induct him into membership of the department.[2]

The presuppositions of the members are further diversified by the increased specialisation of disciplines on which we have already commented and by the wider range of social background of the members. This is not only a reflection of the broadening basis of the class structure of university intake; it also results from the greater diversity of the population. This has wider implications. The traditional university existed in a traditional society, and therefore the norms of the outside world and those of the university harmonised. Similarly in the modern world, the university has not been able to remain immune to the vast dislocations that have taken place in social structure, religious belief and philosophy. The university, like any other institution, will be shaped by the impact of the outside world on the perspectives of its members.

This leads to the final aspect of social influence: the impingement of the outside world. This forms, in the case of the modern university, a subject by itself, and is thus made the theme of the following chapter. But it is necessary to introduce some of the facts at this juncture in order to complete the picture of change.

It is to the needs of the outside world that universities have been called upon to respond in terms of expansion of numbers and the development of new subjects. The figures of growth in British universities in recent years require little comment. In 1953–4 there were 80,602 students in British universities. By 1959–60 the number was 104,009. In 1968–9 it had increased to 212,000. In the new academic year starting in October 1969 the figure was probably over 220,000. In the 1950s the universities grew by about a quarter; in the 1960s they doubled.[3]

Such a vast increase in size has obvious implications for the growth and increasing remoteness of administrative bureaucracies, the formalisation of relationships and the development of specialised roles. Of course, the size of universities in Britain has reached nothing like those in the USA, but the rapid rate of change probably has an effect of its own, irrespective of the ultimate size reached. Several of the characteristics of *Gemeinschaft* social forms are features of stability and changelessness over time, irrespective of the size of the unit.

The new demands of state and industry have changed the role of the academic from the scholar whose life revolved around his college to the busy consultant of a variety of outside interests. The fact that the modern academic spends much of his time working with outside organisations must affect his commitment to both his university and his students. Finally, although sources of employment have always made demands on the universities to prepare young men for careers, the demand has changed in kind. When universities prepared candidates for the clergy, or even for the administrative civil service, there was little difference between careers preparation and imparting a culture. Modern employments, however, involve the acquisition of techniques.

We can now contrast the extreme form of the modern university with that of the traditional. Where the latter provided a secure, stable, but essentially confining social environment, the former is in a state of flux, departmentalised, specialised, but leaving the individual more freedom. It is the usual dilemma between suffocating stability and liberating alienation.

MODEL AND REALITY

These are the models. They are drawn partly from observed fact and partly on theoretical generalisation, and are therefore no more than idealised models. How closely in fact does the image of liberated alienation suit the contemporary British university? We have concentrated on the elements that support the model; we must now examine the exceptions.

First, the continuity of tradition must be noted. There is a desire by all but the most privatised to maintain something of the continuity of the old patterns. This is evident, not only in the ineffective cultivation of synthetic tradition by new institutions but also in the determination to maintain personal tuition and elements of corporate life in the university. The tutorial system, departmental parties, the survival of halls of residence, the encouragement of student societies and informal staff-student contact, all these features contribute in their way to the maintenance of an ideal of community.

Second, the unreality of the bureaucratic model must be remarked. Although in theory relations in a bureaucratic structure are relations between roles and not persons, and so forth, in practice this rarely remains the case beyond the most tangential levels of contact. Whenever individuals work together with any frequency, their relationship is almost certain to become more than formal; personalities will intrude, and affections and antagonisms will develop.

Finally, no matter how large and bureaucratised an institution is in its whole, a range of small face-to-face groups will develop at different points throughout its structure. Thus networks of friends and small groups with common interests and pursuits will be found both within and cutting across formal barriers of rank and department.

It is therefore an exaggeration to regard the modern British university as an alienated institution. Indeed, it is quite likely that the combination of close-knit peer-groups

173

and a wide degree of personal freedom that characterises the life of the modern student or university teacher presents one of the better combinations of those mutually constraining aspects of life – community membership and individual liberty – currently available.

Nevertheless, the growth of the large university does introduce certain elements of strain, loneliness, impersonality and bureaucratic complexity that create difficulties. These difficulties arise because, in the first place, such relationships leave the personality essentially dissatisfied and unfulfilled. This will be particularly important to students, whose previous relational experience has usually been that of school, family and friends. But secondly, there is added strain in that the model of the traditional academic community described above still looms very large in the minds of the inhabitants of universities. Indeed, as it sinks further into the twilight of memory, its nostalgic glow will become yet more rosy, warm and unreal.

We are, it must be remembered, talking of ideal types; the traditional university is not suddenly transformed into a burgeoning multi-varsity. The changes have been making their presence felt gradually but insistently over a large number of years; indeed, since the initial incursion of modern scientific knowledge into their teaching, and definitely since the founding of the "red-brick" universities of the past century. But it is probably true that universities were protected longer from the changes that have overtaken such other aspects of life as residential areas, industrial occupation and government service, because they have a certain institutionalised protection from external influence.

Not only that, but the ideal of the "liberal education"[4] developed in the 19th century by Newman and others made possible a rationale for the continuation of the traditions of the university in a world that was otherwise becoming subjected increasingly to the utilitarian logic of commercial and industrial enterprise. Indeed, such traditions remain strong and firm today, and the Robbins Report[5] tried to root them firmly in the most contemporary thinking.

It is therefore probably valid to speak of an acceleration of an on-going process of change in the past few years, with the immensely increased rate of expansion that these years have seen. This expansion has not only greatly increased the strain on universities and intensified the bureaucratic trend. They have also brought to bear the pressures of the outside world in a newly aggressive way (see Chapter Seven). Finally, the changes have led to a vastly increased self-consciousness by universities and the persons concerned with them. A deep questioning of purpose and function is in progress.

Boris Ford has complained that: "The *quidditas* of universities, to make use of Stephen Daedalus's terminology, is a topic which most of us who work in them seem content to avoid",[6] but even if there is a lack of evidence of serious requestioning, there is a good deal of evidence of disquiet. The Black Papers,[7] which of course go beyond the universities in their scope, can partly be seen as a reaction against changes which are not fully understood and whose wider implications cannot be foreseen. The changes about which this group is concerned mostly relate to increased student numbers and the inevitable transition this implies from the university as an academy of the élite to the concept of mass education. A further area of concern relates to the changing kind of study being carried on, both in terms of education and in terms of research. Boris Ford quotes the concept of the university teacher's vocation elaborated by Sir Eric Ashby:

"The prime responsibility of a university teacher is . . . to diminish ignorance, both his own and that of his pupils . . . our duty is to perpetuate the stability of tradition coupled with the potential for changing tradition; to transmit a corpus of orthodoxy coupled with a technique for constructive dissent from orthodoxy."[8]

As Ford comments, this concept is based on the tradition of disinterested and rigorous critical intelligence that has accompanied the rise of the natural sciences over the past 80 years, although one also detects in it the strains of an earlier view of scholarship as the nurture of traditional knowledge.

How does such a concept fare with the rise of the new technological universities, built round an ideal of co-operation with industry and the preparation of students for particular careers? Can the self-confident *apologia* of universities continue to rest on disinterested rigour and free critical inquiry when an increasing number of them are prepared to accept explicitly such a large degree of heteronomy?

In a different way, the concept of disinterested rigour also incurs criticism from advocates of a renewed spontaneity in academic life, those who see one of the primary goals of a university neither in terms of critical intellectual inquiry nor of a service function for industry, but as a place where people may learn to relate to each other and develop as free self-conscious beings. This has mainly been a theme of the student movement, but nevertheless it has been asserted with sufficent vigour to engage the attention of at least some persons in the universities.

We must now place into this context of change the modern student, and indeed the modern young lecturer. The first point to note is that they are unlikely to have a great deal of sympathy for the traditional university. The traditional university is in decline. Many of our institutions are new, and we have discussed how changes have affected the old, even ancient, foundations as well. And with the mood of self-questioning that accompanies the change, the universities lack the self-confidence and quiet arrogance that are crucial to the assertion of tradition.

But beyond this, traditional appeals are not in keeping with certain modern attitudes and values, where emphasis is placed on change, newness and modernisation. This is particularly the case in that area of culture in which modern youth is most likely to be influenced. Youth culture is one of temporariness, rapidly changing fashion, a general non-ideological disrespect for established authority. Such developments are characteristic of a period of change.

In a static society, the most knowledgeable will tend to be the eldest – the elders – because the only knowledge is that of experience or that handed down from the past. It is in such

176

circumstances that tradition thrives. In a society marked by change, new knowledge develops, old methods are subjected to ruthless inquiry and are unlikely to survive unless they are extremely powerful or can rationalise their position according to the criteria of utility.

But if there is dissatisfaction with what remains of the traditional university community, disillusion with modern bureaucracy is, as we saw in the previous chapter, more complete. Students complain often and bitterly of depersonalisation, of facelessness, of chronic unfulfilment in the contemporary university. Are they seeking the unattainable? Is it not the case that, given the large degree of personal freedom they seek, they will be unable to find the close reassurance for which they sometimes also yearn and which cannot be provided outside the context of a more restricted environment?

Such contradictions do appear with great frequency in the complaints of students and some academics. The latter will claim the complete independence of professional men and will express great wrath at any attempts to proscribe the limits of their freedom, while at the same time they bemoan the loss of academic community that has come in the wake of modern developments. Students will similarly reject paternalism while demanding that the academic staff devote vast periods of time to satisfying their personal and emotional, as well as their intellectual, needs. They will reject the controlled environment of the hall of residence, but complain at the lack of community atmosphere.

These contradictions closely parallel the contradictions in the attitude to authority that we discussed on similar lines in the previous chapter. It may well be the case that a certain degree of alienation is the inevitable result of personal freedom.

COMMUNITY AND FREEDOM

But there are two major, and very different, ways in which the pure polarity between *Gemeinschaft* and *Gesellschaft* do not

177

represent the only available options. First, community and freedom are not entirely mutually exclusive. Second, traditional community and rationalised bureaucracy are not the only available forms of human organisation. We shall deal with each of these in turn.

We have already seen above how elements of primary ties and close-knit personal groups are able to survive in the context of growing rationalisation and bureaucracy. This point can be taken further. Students are often demanding, in their complaint about the modern university, a greater sense of personal involvement in their courses, a greater amount of personal contact, and a lessening of administrative restrictiveness. Much can be done on these lines within the context of the large modern university. There is scope for closer involvement by students in the selection of their courses and in the content of those courses, the means of assessment, and teaching methods.

For example, unit systems of course design and their corresponding means of assessment make possible a greater degree of personal influence by the student on his education, and may thereby reduce feelings of depersonalisation and powerlessness. The development of joint honours degrees, spanning specialisms, may also be of value in ending the fragmentation that can take place in the large university of atomised modern disciplines, although there is frequently a danger that joint degrees simply become not particularly sophisticated mixtures of two different degrees, with little positive integration.

Two important attempts to face up to this problem have been at the Universities of Keele and Sussex. At Keele the attempt to come to terms with the need for both a common core of knowledge and a fair degree of specialism led to the bold and successful development of a four-year degree course. At Sussex boldness has taken a different but equally interesting direction; subject-departments as such are replaced by schools which comprise a group of related interdisciplinary studies. At a different level, the development of collegiate structures and groupings, greater staff-student contact at departmental level, and especially social contact between them, can overcome impersonality.

Similarly, the operation of administrative bureaucracy can be examined to ensure that it confronts students and staff with a humane, understandable visage. Just as in the last chapter we saw how such measures as communications, consultation and representation can offset the student's confrontation with authority as such, so this whole range of other measures can be used to offset the wider problem of social contact and the fabric of relationships.

Behind this whole question stands a paradox. Essential to the traditional university, and indeed to the modern university in so far as it is distinguished from some other large modern institutions, is the implicitness, the quiet acceptance, of norms and codes of behaviour. One of the principal effects of modernisation and rationalisation is an insistence on explicitness, on making things clear and plain. In some ways it is this increasing explicitness and clarity that leads to the impersonality and formalism; such, for example, is the case with the importance of clearly designated and precisely defined roles in a bureaucracy. But here lies the paradox. It is only through a further extension of such explicitness that a tissue of personal relations can be preserved, although such an attempt will always run the risk of making matters worse through routinisation and undue regularity. We have mentioned here some of the areas where this process may take place, not in order to provide a full discussion of the merits and demerits of certain likely educational developments, but to point out the way in which this thinking can be used.

In sum, it is being argued that a humane and involved community can, within certain limits, be protected and carried safely through the great changes taking place in the structure of universities. But this can be done only if careful attention is given to the social implications of educational developments. Changes in courses, teaching methods, examinations and so on, may have a crucial effect on the social structure of the university. This effect has to be among the

179

factors that are taken into account when these changes are planned.

This then is one of the ways in which the demand for involvement can be treated. This is the involvement of the close-knit community to a certain degree; it is that necessary element of personal fulfilment that most people seek from their life and work. It is emotional, to a point, but it is also quiet and mundane. It is at this point that we meet the great contrast with the second way in which our discussion departs from the simple dichotomy of community and bureaucracy.

CONCLUSION: A REVOLUTIONARY COMMUNITY?

In the preceding chapter we noted how the new left in the universities was antipathetic to both traditional and modern bureaucratic modes of academic authority, and suggested that the category of charisma may assist us in a fuller understanding of the kind of authority structure that emerges as a counter to existing forms in the course of a protest movement. In the case of both traditional and bureaucratic forms of authority, we can readily find general forms of social relationships to which they correspond. Thus, in somewhat rough and ready fashion, we can equate traditional authority patterns with the collegiate community of academic scholarship; and bureaucratic forms can be related to the modern departmentalised and research-oriented university. The parallels between the two will have been evident throughout this chapter, and they do not need to be spelt out here in more detail.

But what form of social relationships corresponds to this charismatic form of authority? One central problem here is the elusiveness of charisma and its intrinsic transience. It has rarely been a substantive base for the on-going operation of an institution, since essential to it is the denigration of institutionalisation, structuring and continuity. Thus in practice charismatic authorities very rapidly become transformed into either bureaucracies, some of the various forms of traditional authority, or a combination of both.

Nevertheless, if we use charisma as an ideal type, we do not expect organisations to be entirely characterised by its operation, just as bureaucratic and traditional authority rarely appear in their purest form. We shall be content to identify an element of charisma, which will be present or absent in a more or less important degree. Therefore, given this fact and given the fact that the student left approaches the charismatic, what can be said to characterise or typify the texture of social relationships and perspectives of protest groups?

In the literature of both the new left and those who have written about them the expression "community" appears with great regularity. They complain that community has disappeared from relationships in the modern academy; they claim to have restored community relationships within their own groups and in the course of their on-going protests. Indeed, as we have seen, the creation of such a "community" forms part of the *raison d'être* of such protests. Discussion with the new left on the subject of their view of the ideal university soon reveals that it has something to do with the creation of an establishment where people come to know each other as the fellow members of a community. But this is deceptive.

As we have seen, community relationships are characteristic of the traditional university, or more mundanely they may appear as the fabric of informal but well-rooted friendships that exist in virtually any institution. The new left is, of course, as opposed to traditional authority as it is to modern bureaucratic forms, and some of the protests at the University of Oxford, one of the few places where this authority still impinges on university life to any great degree, have demonstrated this. It would therefore be surprising if the new left's rhetoric of community were capable of being translated into a plea for a return to settled traditional universities.

The point is that the form of authority most frequently contacted by student protest, and that form which corresponds most closely to the whole range of political and social changes which have given birth to the new left's protest, is modern bureaucratic authority. Naturally, therefore, the student left has tended to strike its attitudes in opposition to this type of authority. Since the language of opposition to bureaucracy and rationalised procedure tends to be couched in terms of its normal polarity – that of traditional community – a misleading impression is given. If we examine the particular complaints of the new left against the modern university more closely we shall see that it only occasionally differs on the same grounds as does the traditional university.

George Benello,[9] a Canadian academic and supporter of the new left, has attempted to tackle this problem in an essay which shows a remarkable lack of dogmatism and an acute awareness of the difficulties. He starts with an analysis of the decline of community that rests largely on conservative thinkers; it is significant that the title of his essay, "Wasteland Culture", is taken from T. S. Eliot. But he then introduces the rhetoric of the left and sees this decline in community in terms of a fairly orthodox Marxist explanation. He next faces the problem of the traditional and conservative implications of *Gemeinschaft*.

"[the assumption that] to speak of *gemeinschaft* and other aspects of psychic and communal wholeness is first of all to go back to the past, into a pre-technological Garden of Eden, and secondly to reintroduce all the old forms of coercion: the church, the aristocracy, and also the narrowness and stultification of pre-industrial rural life. But the past is only relevant when it gives examples of organic institutions suited to human needs; the guild, as opposed to the modern labor union would be one such. As with cities, which before technology could be unplanned but aesthetically harmonious and pleasing, and functional, so we must reintegrate a social fabric which technology and its instrumentalities has torn apart. In part we are dealing with the Rousseauistic belief which was the basis of the French Revolution. Tear apart all the old institutions which keep man in bonds and replace them with overall institutions – for Rousseau the state – coordinated mystically via the General Will, and now by the market system, in the West, or in the East by a totalitarianism which speaks in the name of the proletariat."[10]

In terms of social action rather than written ideology, the aspect of student protest which has asserted this communitarian desire more than any other is the concept of protest as end-in-itself and the free university, both of which ideas we have discussed in some detail in Chapters Two to Four. It is in these concepts that we can most easily see the nature of the communitarian demand and thereby make contrasts between it and both the traditional or *Gemeinschaft* form and the bureaucratic or *Gesellschaft*. The following is an attempt to capture most of the important elements of this contrast in so far as they concern the special institutional case of the British university:

CHARACTERISTICS OF TYPICAL MODELS OF IDEALISED UNIVERSITIES

Traditional	Modern	Revolutionary
Small	Large	Small
Static, stable	Changing	Changing
Structured according to traditional practice	Structured according to rational efficiency	Unstructured
Primary ties; commensality, shared life of entrenched custom	Secondary ties; professionalised	Primary ties; shared life of intensity
Status distinctions legitimised by tradition, and tending to correspond to erudition and scholarship	Status distinctions of (i) administrative hierarchy and (ii) academic merit	No accepted status distinctions, but emergent leadership
Common presuppositions and values resulting from narrow stratum of recruitment and shared values	Varied backgrounds and values; no prior ethical or religious commitment required	Common values as members of a revolutionary group
Turned in upon itself away from the world; monastic	Implicated in wide range of external concerns	Suspicious of world but seeking to conquer or convert it
Scholarship	Research	The lessons of experience in revolutionary action
Overlapping roles	Division of labour	Existentialist concept of totality of person and role
Transmission of common core of culture	Education in specialised skills	Self-awareness and revolutionary critique through work for the revolution

The relationship between the idea of the activist community and that of charismatic authority in the revolutionary group discussed in Chapter Five should be clear. The challenge to authority posed by the new left in the universities, and the forms of social solidarity and action which they seek, are of the same inspiration. The activist community represents the network of relationships implied by charismatic authority. They both relate to similar problems of change within the university, the decline of the traditional and the disillusion with the emerging modern university. They relate to a similar concern to go behind the forms that appear to mask bureaucratic authority in order to seek a total morality, a continuous ethical critique and questioning. They are also related to the same pessimism about the possibility of achieving objectives through "normal" channels of rational discussion, constitutional pressure and emotive restraint. The models of charisma and the activist community counter the implications of such a mode of political action at every point.

Of course, the university is here but a special case of a wider problem. In our discussion of this matter, and in the reference to Benello's essay, we have already been forced to go beyond the university framework. The university is an institution where the apparent decline of community can be grasped more easily, precisely because the university lays certain claims to being a community. It is an institution where the suffocating effect on "normal" political procedures of modern economy and technology can be protested against more loudly, precisely because the university lays certain claims to autonomy. It is therefore impossible to proceed further in our discussion without looking beyond the university as such. We shall reach this position by way of a discussion of the relationship between the university and the world. This lies at the root of much of the radical's unrest and contempt for the university as an institution.

REFERENCES

1. Toennies, F., *Gemeinschaft und Gesellschaft* (translated into English by Loomis, C. P., *Community and Association*)
2. Chester, R., "Role Conflict and the Junior Academic" (in Martin, D. (ed.), *Anarchy and Culture*, 1969)
3. Vaizey, J., "The Numbers Game: How Many Students?" (*New Statesman*, 17 October 1969)
4. Newman, J. H., *The Idea of a University*, 1893
5. Report of Committee on Higher Education, 1963
6. Ford, B., "What is a University?" (*New Statesman*, 24 October 1969)
7. Black Papers on Education, Numbers 1 and 2, *Critical Quarterly*, 1969
8. Ford, B., *op cit*
9. Benello, C. G., "Wasteland Culture" (in McGuigan, G. F. (ed.), *Student Protest*, 1968)
10. *ibid*, p 204

CHAPTER SEVEN

The University and the World

"A university has other objectives besides providing industry with ready-made recruits and much has already been done to promote closer collaboration with industry. But . . . it would be valuable if the Universities collectively made a further deliberate and determined effort to gear a larger part of their 'output' to the economic and industrial needs of the nation. . . . There are also a good many comments from Industry which reveal a gap between what the postgraduate studies have traditionally provided and what Industry would like to receive . . . (a) a shift in postgraduate effort from the more traditional types of course to something which is avowedly more 'vocational' and often shorter in duration; (b) training methods designed to ease the transition from the academic to the industrial world."

(University Grants Committee, Memorandum of General Guidance, 1967–72.)

Such is the importance to the development of new-left student ideology of the changing relationship between the university and the instruments of state and economy that we have had occasion to refer to it at several points. It is now time to concentrate on this question in so far as it deals with the implications for academic freedom of certain contemporary changes in the university and its relationship with other institutions.

The debate on the kind of links which ought to exist between the university and other institutions obviously goes far beyond the problem of the new left, and is an issue of wider importance than the student movement itself. We shall here consider some of the substantive issues involved, and go on to set the perspective of student militants in the context of other attempts to come to grips with these problems. A point of striking importance in this whole debate is that it cuts right across conventional political differences.

DEVELOPMENTS SINCE ROBBINS

Two major and related developments confront British universities at the present time. First is the commitment to the Robbins Report[1] recommendation that entrance to higher education be assured to a fixed proportion of qualified school leavers, which it is now realised will involve far higher numbers than Robbins had predicted. It is estimated that by 1980 places will have to be found for 30 per cent of the school leavers' age-groups, compared with the present proportion of 15 per cent.[2]

Second is the increasingly insistent demand by the state and industry both for research facilities in the universities and for young people prepared for specific occupations which match the needs of employers. These developments raise implications for the overall structure of higher education (at present based on the distinction of the "binary" system between the autonomous universities and colleges of technology in the local authority sector) for the autonomy of the universities (exemplified in the changing role of the University Grants Committee) and for the internal structure of institutions.

The Robbins Report tried to achieve a balanced position in relation to the various pressures that exist. The report was a fine example of the major tradition of British liberal education, coupling a firm belief in education as a valid end in itself with concern for the needs of industry, commerce and administration. Robbins[3] identified four objectives "essential to any properly balanced system" of higher education. First was "instruction in skills suitable to play a part in the general division of labour". The committee put this first, not necessarily because it was the most important, but because it was

187

often forgotten; it was folly to assume that the majority of men undertook education for motives entirely unconnected with future occupation and reward. Second:

"while emphasising that there is no betrayal of values when institutions of higher education teach what will be of some practical use, we must postulate that what is taught should be taught in such a way as to promote the general powers of the mind. The aim should be to produce not mere specialists but rather cultivated men and women."

Third, the Committee mentioned the advancement of learning, and finally, if the second point may have been an expression of a faith in élite culture, in its fourth objective the Committee displayed its democratic credentials:

"Finally there is a function that is more difficult to describe concisely, but that is none the less fundamental: the transmission of a common culture and common standards of citizenship. . . . It is not merely by providing places for students of all classes that [the ideal of equality of opportunity] will be achieved, but also by providing, in the atmosphere of the institutions in which the students live and work, influences that in some measure compensate for any inequalities of home background."

A further important feature of the Robbins Report was that it sought to base its recommendations for expansion, not on the needs of the economy, but on the "pool of ability" available. Robbins[4] was opposed to a binary concept of education in which the "élite" (university) sector would remain in rigid separation from the other (college of technology) sector. It sought to provide a flexible but university-oriented system under which all technical institutions would be given the potential to become universities, and where they should all cultivate close links with existing universities. In other words, there would be a system of stratification, but it would be an open system with the possibility of much social mobility, rather than a closed structure of hereditary estates. By keeping the universities as the peak

188

of this system, it can be expected that mobility would take the form of becoming "more like" a university.

Since the Robbins Report there have been several crucial developments which have affected its delicate balance. First, the prospect of vastly increased numbers referred to above calls into question the ability of existing institutions, and the assumptions of these institutions, to cope with the demands which will be made upon them. If expansions of expenditure fail to keep abreast of the increase in numbers, what changes will be required of institutions to accommodate the new numbers? What shifts will there be in the balance of numbers between the different types of institution? What changes will be demanded in the operations of institutions given the inevitable intrusion of notions of efficiency and productivity?

A further blow was struck at the Robbins balance when the Government[5] rejected its solution for the division between universities and colleges of higher education. The motivations behind a "binary" system are mixed, as will be considered later, but an important implication of the decision was that the university model should not become generalised for all higher education. In particular this undermined the concepts of autonomy and of monasticism.

Third, the Dainton[6] Report, which dealt with the career preparation of scientific, industrial and other personnel, took a different attitude to the question of the determination of subject balance.[7] An important factor in this was no doubt the swing away from technological subjects in the choice of new university entrants. There is therefore a possibility that the *laissez faire* attitude of Robbins towards the relationship between student demand and course provision will be endangered.

Of course, one must be careful not to exaggerate this apparent move towards vocationalism. A system of higher education which bore no relation whatsoever to the kind of occupation likely to be undertaken by its students would be difficult to justify. Further, universities have always played a vocational role. In medieval times they concentrated their

189

attention on the church and, to a lesser extent, law and medicine. In a more recent period they have cultivated a particular type of administrative preparation, that which is most
typically found in the civil servant of the administrative
grade who has read Greats at Oxford. But in these cases the
university provided a broad education which was then applied to particular vocations. Now the emphasis is increasingly on the design of courses which will tailor a student to a
particular set of needs articulated by industrial institutions.
The imperatives of the potential employer may sometimes
assume a more powerful, and more narrowly conceived, role;
though the effect of this change is somewhat moderated by
the evidence that competence in the modern industrial structure requires a reasonable amount of general intelligence and
knowledge.

Boris Ford[8] has drawn attention to the difficulty experienced by these new institutions in expressing their concept of a university. He quotes the charter of the University
of Bradford:

"The objects of the University shall be the advancement
of learning and knowledge and the application of knowledge to human welfare and in particular (although without prejudice to the generality of the foregoing) study and
research in science and technology and collaboration for
the furtherance of these objects with industry, commerce,
the professions and other institutions."

and the Vice-Chancellor of Brunel University:

"We are trying to provide an industry-oriented or
directed education, having in mind the national need for
technologists and the sort of society in which our graduates
will be living and working. This is not the acceptance, as
an end, of a narrow vocational education; rather our aim
is to devise a mode of education for technologists that will
satisfy the broad educational aims that men accept today
and to use the technological subjects as a means. If you
wish to call us pragmatic, that would not be unfair."

It is as yet impossible to say exactly how existing concepts of academic autonomy and of the nature of intellectual endeavour will be affected by these transformations. How possible will it be in practice to maintain a balance between the traditional concerns of liberal higher education and aggressive vocationalism?

Related to these pressures is one about which we know even less: the influence of industrial sponsorship of research over academic freedom. When a group of students interrupts a lecture the nation's press howls abuse at their disregard for this sacred principle. But it is likely that every day this freedom is being more successfully undermined, and on a far greater scale, by industrial intervention. But we do not know the facts, nor are we in a position to pronounce on their significance.

Finally, changes of immense importance will result from the changing role of the UGC and other aspects of policy which demonstrate the increasing desire by governments to exercise more detailed control over university affairs. The quotation at the head of this chapter provides a bald and succinct statement of the direction in which the UGC is attempting to steer the universities, and the policy is still in its infancy.

Again, the facts on the degree of control the UGC exercises over the actions of individual institutions are shrouded in mystery. In 1969 the journal *Universities Quarterly*[9] sought to commission a comprehensive series of articles on the UGC. In the event, only four articles were produced; in other areas the necessary data were impossible to obtain. Among those which were written was one by A. H. Halsey, which drew attention to a crucial factor in the determination of this development: the changing sources of university incomes over the past half-century.

The following table, taken from Halsey,[10] indicates both (i) the growing proportion of the universities' income provided by the state, and (ii) the rising absolute size of this contribution. The universities are no longer marginal consumers of public expenditure whose dependence on the state is only partial:

191

SOURCES OF UNIVERSITY INCOME FOR SELECTED YEARS SINCE 1920

Year	Total income of universities	Analysis by source in per cent of total income					
		Parliamentary grants	Grants from Local Authorities	Fees	Endowments	Donations and subscriptions	Other sources
	£						
1920–21	3,020,499	33·6	9·3	33·0	11·2	2·7	3·3
1923–24	3,587,366	35·5	12·0	33·6	11·6	2·5	4·8
1928–29	5,174,510	35·9	10·1	27·8	13·9	2·4	6·9
1933–34	5,953,320	35·1	9·2	32·8	13·7	2·4	6·8
1938–39	6,712,067	35·8	9·0	29·8	15·4	2·6	7·4
1946–47	13,043,541	52·7	5·6	23·2	9·3	2·2	7·0
1949–50	22,009,735	63·9	4·6	17·7	5·7	1·7	6·4
1953–54	31,112,024	70·5	3·6	12·0	4·3	1·6	8·0
1955–56	36,894,000	72·7	3·1	10·8	3·8	0·9	8·7
1961–62	74,113,000	76·5	2·1	9·0	2·7	0·9	8·9
1966–67	189,183,000	82·7	0·2	7·0	1·4	0·5	7·4

Halsey provides a necessary reminder that the state has intervened in the universities at crucial intervals since the Middle Ages and that the effect has more often than not been in the interests of intellectual advance. He also demonstrates the success that has been enjoyed by the UGC for fifty years in providing a valid buffer between state and academy which was acknowledged by both parties. But, he says, times change:

"On the one hand the claimants to power and participation in state and society have changed and the question therefore becomes who are the power wielders and, more specifically, who exercises what kind of power in, over and through the University Grants Committee? On the other hand, the expansion of university studies, especially in the natural and applied sciences (to which more recently must be added a tremendous growth of the social sciences) has almost completely eroded the financial basis of autonomy, converting the universities into state dependencies and thus placing the burden of maintaining academic freedom on the beliefs and sentiments of those who wield power in the modern systems of government and administration."[11]

The great unsolved questions which are obviously raised by such an analysis are, first, how far has this process gone and what are its practical, as opposed to theoretical, challenges to autonomy? And, second, how strong are "beliefs and sentiments" against the power of the purse and the authority of the state?

THE IVORY TOWER

We may now consider some of the most important attitudes which have developed among those concerned with higher education in relation to this changing role of the university. First, we may distinguish the ivory tower concept, which opposes all or most links with other institutions on the grounds that the pursuit of knowledge is a thing unto itself, carried on for its own sake. It follows from this view that knowledge and its pursuit should not be subject to external criteria, such as its contribution to productivity or a responsibility to create social and political awareness. This view of the role of the academy is of considerable vintage and the respect in which it is often held is a mark of the success of the academic sector in having itself marked off as a special status group, entitled to certain exemptions from involvement in national economic life. Academic life is here seen as that of a religious order rather than as a service activity for the modern economy. This is, however, the approach to education that is criticised by "modernisers" as "outmoded", because it insists on cultivating such pursuits as the study of the classics which make no contribution to economic and social progress, and other proclaimed objectives.

Surprisingly, it is the development of the modern economy and its gargantuan claims over other institutions that gives the ivory tower a new rationale. If the criteria of efficiency and contribution to resolving the balance of payments deficit are increasingly to dominate wider areas of society, it may be considered of value to preserve and protect "islands" in which other criteria and values may flourish. This may seem necessary for the protection of variety, choice and pluralism. However, it is unlikely that this argument will be used to justify the existence of the whole structure of university education. The consumption of intellectual and financial resources by the universities, and the demand by society for trained manpower, are such that universities are bound to be called upon to make a wider contribution than the cultivation of their own gardens for their own amusement.

The ivory tower is thus likely to be used as an argument in favour of an enclave within the educational system rather than a call for the entire educational sector to be such an enclave. This distinction is important, and will arise again in the course of this discussion.

The ivory tower is able to sustain itself because

(i) a large proportion of its activities comprises the culture of the society's élite, who are therefore inclined to protect it. In Britain at any rate it has been the case that even when industrial entrepreneurs have been rugged utilitarians, their sons or their grandsons have sought to use their wealth to take their place in the traditional structure of social status. In part this has meant acquiring élite culture.

(ii) Over the centuries the ivory tower has successfully surrounded itself with an aura of tradition and sanctity. Respect for learning, for the written word, often for books themselves as objects, is deeply entrenched in the history of many societies; in Britain it co-exists with a general tendency to despise "intellectuals" and to regard academics as absent-minded, benign figures of fun.

This aura of sanctity has received impetus from an unsuspected quarter in that the new importance of education to social and occupational mobility and to the development of modern technology has led to a renewal of the respect in which learning *per se* is held. Although these views of the role of education are far removed from the ivory tower, they do assist the educational sector to maintain a place of prestige that is essential to the success of the claim to special status that the ivory tower demands. By and large universities in Britain have asserted their right to be considered institutions somewhat apart from the wider society; to be revered if occasionally ridiculed, respected if occasionally suspected. It is this pervading atmosphere that helps explain the vast interest in and anger over student disruptions; engaging in physical protest within a university invokes something of the horror that would be created by similar occurrences in church.

THE TRADITION OF LIBERAL CRITICISM

Partly related and partly opposed to the ivory tower concept of the university is that which sees it as a centre for intellectual and social criticism. This concept has been very well expressed by Sir Eric Ashby, speaking specifically of the situation of the contemporary student in an oration delivered at the London School of Economics a full two years before protest exploded there. This passage has been much quoted by student radicals asserting that times, and their own situation, have changed:

"The paradigm for a graduate forty years ago was the conventional man, ready to take responsibility for preserving a set of values which he felt no need to question, deferring to his elders because they were older, not because they were wiser, obedient to principles, constitutions, traditions. That sort of young man cannot cope with the flux of the modern world. The contemporary paradigm is a man educated for insecurity, who can innovate, improvise, solve problems with no precedent. He must have expert knowledge. That is what he gets from his lectures and laboratories. He must also have the confidence which comes from participation in community living. That is what he gets from belonging, as a co-equal, to a society of Chancellor, Masters and Scholars." [12]

This is related to the ivory tower partly because élite culture, at least in Britain, implies in part liberal education, which in turn implies a certain (albeit restrained) readiness to be critical of existing institutions and beliefs and a willingness to be inquiring and tolerant of new ideas. The conservative element within the British cultural élite will place its emphasis on those aspects of that culture which stress the continuity of established values, while the liberal wing places its emphasis on the virtues of an independent mind in criticism and scrutiny. This is also related to the ivory tower view in that detached criticism can only be the product of an education system which is largely free from external control.

If external institutions, whether they be state or private, keep control over an education system in its detailed activities, such criticism will not be able to flourish. The strictly utilitarian university may be able to make use of the results of such social criticism, but it will be unable to create the conditions in which it takes place, unless for its own wider ends it is prepared to permit the existence of islands of intellectual autonomy. Such is the problem of the scientist in the USSR, who has to be given autonomy in certain specialised non-political areas of thought, and who in consequence becomes a potentially dangerous free-thinker in other areas of life.

Intellectual innovation and useful criticism therefore depend on an atmosphere of freedom for academics; and freedom must imply the freedom not to produce anything of utility, the freedom to be wrong, the freedom to pursue interests that no one else finds of any value. Thus the advocate of the tradition of socially useful academic criticism will see the autonomy of the ivory tower as a by-product, probably a congenial by-product, of society's own "best interest". The defender of the ivory tower, on the other hand, will see useful social criticism and innovation as a by-product of his major pre-occupation – the pursuit of knowledge in its own cause.

But the school of liberal criticism diverges from the ivory tower in so far as, while rejecting constraints imposed by the wider society on knowledge, it stresses the contribution knowledge can make to that society. The advocate of critical liberal education is likely to state his defence, not on the grounds of education for education's sake, but on the case that society cannot change and improve without new ideas, whether within the technological developments arising from study of the natural sciences or in political and social changes related to the humanities and social sciences.

Related to both these concepts of the role of the university is an argument which is concerned mainly with the actual task of education as opposed to the somewhat different concept of the pursuit of knowledge which we have so far bracketed under the general term "education". This is the argument that education is in some way a right; that if a man (or, increasingly, a woman) has the ability to develop his mind to a certain level with the assistance of educational institutions, he should be able to do so. This was the view of education adopted by the Robbins Report, which, while recognising the contribution education had to make to the economy, insisted that this should not be the primary rationale for an expansion in the universities:

". . . education ministers intimately to ultimate ends, in developing man's capacity to understand, to contemplate and to create. And it is a characteristic of the aspirations of this age to feel that, where there is capacity to pursue such activities, there that capacity should be fostered. The good society desires equality of opportunity for its citizens to become not merely good producers but also good men and women." [13]

This is remarkable in that the concept of education as a right for all with ability is a refreshingly generous and liberal argument for a Royal Commission to use in attempting to influence HM Government; whether or not this has been the main motive of Governments in accepting most of the Robbins recommendations is another matter. The point reflects how deeply rooted the liberal concept of education has become. Despite the equally deep-rooted utilitarianism and anti-intellectualism in our national traditions, purely vocational education has never been popular among English educators, even though there have been persistent and powerful attempts at instituting it, particularly for the lower classes, at all levels of the education system. In nearly every case the teachers within the schools and institutes have insisted on leavening the rigours of vocationalism with what is now known as "liberal studies" or what in an earlier period was usually the study of classical languages, history and geography.

Whether this has been adequately or outrageously taught, and whether it has resulted from a simple desire to ape the trappings of high culture and thereby acquire social status, is immaterial. The feature has been a crucial one in the development of educational ideas, at least among educators and the cultural élite, in Britain.

One can detect similar processes in the continuing struggle between the two halves of the "binary system" of higher education, as the technical colleges seek to make their courses resemble those of the university and vigorously try to avoid becoming type-cast as academies of job-preparation. This is a question to which we shall later return.

CRYPTO-MARXISM

A further approach to universities and education which takes a "dark" view of involvement with other institutions is the crypto-Marxist view. One is here using "Marxist" in a special and extremely vague sense, referring merely to suspicion of the role of industry and state and the view that their influence on an institution is *prima facie* sinister and corrupting.

This attitude is by no means limited to those who would dub themselves Marxists. Nor again do all Marxists take such a view; those whose model of Marxist society is to be found in the USSR, Cuba or China are very much in favour of such intervention when it is carried out by the governments of those societies. Nevertheless, in a society such as ours those most likely to be suspicious of governmental and (particularly) industrial involvement are likely to be those who are under at least a residual Marxist influence.*

* Important exceptions are those who see something sinister in government intervention, but welcome that of industry. These critics are those whose image of capitalist enterprise is fixed on the period of a myriad of competing small firms, rather than the giants of modern industry.

People who take this point of view probably do not hold that all connections between the universities and the outside world are in themselves a distortion of knowledge, but they are fearful of its potential implications. They see much cause for concern in the increasingly vocational role of education and feel that education is being misused if it becomes simply a tool whereby industrialists prepare and produce their obedient new recruits. (On the far left this is of course taken much further, leading to a paranoid reaction against all career implications of education; indeed the rejection of the very concept of career.)

Such concern is not limited to the educational aspects of university work; there is also alarm about the kind of research that is carried on in university departments, and the source of the sponsorship. In the USA this issue has come to a head with the vast involvement of many universities with the defence industry; several American universities have come to face the question squarely and have sought to establish certain criteria which must be followed if acceptance of contracted research is to be consonant with ideas of academic freedom. In Britain the issue received considerable attention following the Essex affair with the scientist from Porton Down, and on a smaller scale with the protest at the University of Glasgow concerning a course of lectures on military strategy.

The fears of the liberal or orthodox socialist on this issue are fears that academic autonomy will be eroded by the ability of industrial interests to determine the type of research going on in university departments. There is probably little root and branch opposition to the very idea of industry making use of the knowledge and resources of university departments; given the frame of reference of liberals and reformists who basically accept the structure of existing society, this involvement is likely to be considered innocuous or even desirable. The fear arises when the industrial interest is in a position to control what takes place in a department, to influence the direction of major research into special channels that serve the interests of a particular company or industry, and thus to direct it away from other channels which may be considered, academically or socially, of greater significance. This fear increases when one considers those disciplines which may involve developments with wider social implications, such as chemical and biological warfare, or research into the social sciences. Matters are considered yet more serious when the State appears as the agent of industry, or when the State itself appears to use the university for its own end.

THE NEW LEFT: (i) AGAINST INTERVENTION

In the view of the new left, however, the objection goes further than the liberals' fear of excessive power; there is a belief that the interests of state and industry are not merely too powerful but are *ipso facto* illegitimate and should not receive expression anywhere. Research into defence means, to the new left, research into the means for keeping the populations of Latin America, Asia and Africa subject to exploitation and poverty. Research into counter-insurgency means discovering ways of preventing these same peoples from liberating themselves from this oppression.

Education, which is closely linked to preparation for a particular employment, or a general range of employments, means (in the new left view) preparing people to shrink and twist their personalities until they are suited to fit the slots in the industrial machine that the owners of industry find it in their interests to have other people occupy. Study of such subjects as personnel management is the study of how to manipulate workers and thereby deny them their ability to challenge the authority of a management which exploits them financially and deprives them of their autonomy as human beings.

One can see how fear of the role of powerful institutions can become inflated from the worry of the disconcerted liberal to the paranoic fear of the extreme radical who sees himself surrounded at every turn by instruments of distortion, exploitation and manipulation under the guise of academic freedom. It is not surprising that such persons have little concern for the argument that by disrupting a university campus or interrupting a lecture they are interfering with something precious.

But it is difficult to understand how the extreme opposition to university involvement with some form of career preparation can be justified. It is not sensible to envisage a world in which people do not seek to take advantage of the product of each other's skills, if only in such obvious fields as medicine and food preparation. One also encounters an ambiguity in the left's position here, since it is sometimes the case that, while deploring vocationalism in western education, they will applaud it as crucial to the people's revolution if it occurs in, say, China.[14]

There is a further important difference between the new left and those other approaches to education which are suspicious of state and industrial involvement. Although opposing most forms of interference with the universities, the left does so from such a position that there is little left to defend; if all knowledge is riddled with social biases, what is there of value to be rescued by the universities remaining free of involvement with industry and government? If the left is to make a stand in defence of certain academic values, then it is making exceptions to its image of existing society, and this is a concession which ultimately undermines the distinctiveness of its whole position.

THE NEW LEFT: (ii) FOR INTERVENTION

Turning now to the various arguments which are used to justify the involvement of the universities in the wider world, we must first again consider the revolutionaries. For although the far left opposes existing forms of societal involvement, it does not wish to defend the ivory tower or the university of critical liberal thinkers. The key text for the point of departure of this aspect of their argument is in Marx: "The philosophers have interpreted the world in various ways; the point is to change it."[15] The revolutionary, far from wanting a politically neutral and uninvolved university, seeks one dedicated to the class struggle.

Of course, he is unlikely to believe that he can actually bring this about in the absence of the revolution itself, but by raising the issue within the university he may help the struggle get under way.

A very clear-cut example of this in a British student protest was the LSE Vietnam occupation. Taking over a university building and holding it as a sanctuary for persons involved in the demonstration was very clearly confronting the "bourgeois" conception of the university with the revolutionary conception. The whole affair was very symbolic. The expected battle between the police and the marchers was merely a symbol of the struggle between the USA and the Viet Cong.* The use of the LSE as a sanctuary and field hospital, completely unnecessarily, was a symbol of the role of the revolutionary university. As in all religious ritual, the symbol rehearses a wider reality that cannot otherwise be given expression in the mundane world; but the believers recognise it, respond, and are brought nearer to that reality by participation in the ritual.

It is possible to identify four separate lines of argument that support the new left's concept of the engaged university. First, and most attractive, is the pluralistic argument. If, as we have noted above, some subjects and research are considered to be expressions of a manipulative social structure, then the university has already forfeited its claim to neutrality in subject content. Why therefore should there be outrage at its sheltering activities that are simply biased in another direction? If a university can teach management training, why not also instruct shop stewards in greater militancy? If defence studies, why not courses in urban guerrilla warfare? If a training in social work that trains people to help the poor make the best of their existing situation, why not involvement in community activism? There is a logic in this that must

---

* The expected struggle with the police would also demonstrate the way in which authority the world over is linked and in solidarity; when the struggle did not take place, this was held to be evidence of the dangerously devious ways in which the mystification of bourgeois liberalism operates.

appeal to all who believe that universities should either be neutral or should tolerate within their confines a multiplicity of subjectivities. The issue as framed in this way has, as we have seen, appeared on many American campuses, where demands for such education have in several instances been granted.

But, of course, this argument does not always appear in pluralistic guise; it may well be posed as a challenge to the university, not as to whether it can tolerate within itself a genuine pluralism of values (and that may be a strong enough challenge for many an institution) but in order to make the institution adopt a particular stand as a body. We have drawn attention to this aspect of the argument in connection with several points.

A third and similarly dangerous argument as this last is the familiar plea of all totalitarian movements. Such issues as racialism, Vietnam and exploitation, are so urgent, runs the argument, that there is neither time nor resources that can be indulged in the luxury of academic freedom. All possible resources must be harnessed to the creation of a revolutionary movement, and if in the course of this some institutions like the academic way of life are trampled underfoot, that is a matter of small relevance. This impatience with academic reflection and freedoms masquerades as a manly intolerance of quibbling old fools and thereby forms an essential part of the charismatic claim of the new left to the leadership of the student community. It also opens the way to the suppression of free speech in the interests of "greater objectives". This intolerance is central, though not exclusive, to Marxism as a doctrine of total confidence in one's own righteousness and in the inherent wickedness or folly of rival creeds.

Finally, university involvement in the revolution is justified on the grounds that there can be no education without action. This concept of education by experience comes dangerously close to that of the conservative pragmatist.[16] But, of course, the revolutionary's argument is very different from that of the conservative. We have already discussed the essential ideas in the case. It is based on the belief that the only meaningful learning experience can come from breaking free of the formal structures and innovating in the course of action; it is this innovatory experience that teaches, in contrast with the customary practice from which the conservative claims to derive his empirical wisdom. The idea that wisdom is imparted from the minds of others and thereby handed down is entirely absent from this theory of innovatory experience, except in so far as Marxism itself forms a tradition.

EDUCATION AS A "SOCIAL SERVICE"

But the new left is not alone in advocating a certain kind of societal involvement by universities, just as they were not alone in resisting certain forms of such involvement. One argument, which is far distant from the creed of the new left, states: There is a crying need in the world for the fruits of knowledge. We need people who can plan the economy; engineers who can improve the standard of life through their innovations; experts who can give advice to governments on a whole range of issues in order to ensure that we are more intelligently ruled; teachers willing to educate the new generations; and dedicated workers in the social services. In a changing world we need to advance in knowledge and expertise; in a democratic world we need to use our best intelligences in the service of common ends. Meanwhile, education which leads to good careers can be a vital channel of social mobility, enabling the most able from all backgrounds to compete with those who have the advantages.[17]

This view of the university is likely to attack academic isolationists on several grounds. It regards their attempts at maintaining a high culture as anti-populist elitism; its model of valuable education is likely to be the engineer from a working-class home applying his acquired skills on tasks whose productive contribution can be readily and universally appreciated. This is far removed from the classics scholar cultivating in the solitude of his college the study of a dead language appreciated by only a few and in any case mainly taught in public schools to the sons of the upper classes. In fact, proponents of this view of education are likely to dislike universities as such, and will find their educational ideal in the polytechnics and in the colleges of advanced technology (now known, of course, as technological universities).

One of the most articulate proponents of this approach is Eric Robinson,[18] himself a teacher at the Enfield College of Technology. Robinson does not advocate a system of narrow vocationalism, but he gives the usual debate an interesting and important twist by pitting a vocationally oriented liberal education against what he considers to be the narrow and restrictive academic education characteristic of the universities. For Robinson it is the pursuit of ultimate truth (which he says pervades academic education) which renders it authoritarian, subject- as opposed to student-centred, restrictive of new development and independent thought:

"If liberalism in education means the development of the individual to establish and maintain his own values and to be equipped to hold his own against the pressures around him there has never been a greater need for it than now. But to assume that it is best pursued by ignoring the world as it is and the need to earn a living in this imperfect world is a great mistake. The most illiberal education is the one which makes a student mere fodder for the industrial machine; but the man most vulnerable to the industrial machine is the one who must enter it without knowing or understanding anything about it. To pretend that the real world of 'muck and brass' does not exist is the worst disservice higher education can do a student. The most liberal education he can receive is one which enables him to make his way in employment without being its prisoner, which enables him to serve but also to change industry, which teaches him not only how to use his leisure and how to live in spite of his work but how to make his work an integral part of his life. Our system of higher education fails dismally to provide such education. In its timidity and social conservatism it imposes continual pressure on students to conform and to surrender to social pressures. That is why students are in revolt – not because of the superficialities of institutional organisation or the inadequacies of teaching techniques but because of the basically restrictive conception of the education to which they are subjected." [19]

It is interesting and instructive that this argument is directed equally against academic conservatives cultivating an ivory tower ideal and student radicals seeking to abjure all contact with industry in present society.

THE PRODUCTION-LINE UNIVERSITY

It is occasionally difficult to distinguish this "social service" concept of higher education from a further category: the production-line university. The most cogent expression of this is found in Clarke Kerr's[20] multi-varsity, where the image of the factory represents both the internal structure of the university and the guiding objective of its activities. (It is important to note that Kerr considers this a "democratic" university and contrasts it with "élitist" traditional notions.) But this is an American view, and cannot be considered as a directly relevant concept for our discussion, which is concerned with British problems.

Somewhat similar to it, however, is the view taken by industrialists and their political spokesmen, who see the main task of education as being to prepare men to work under them, and who see the main use of a university's research facilities as extensions of their own laboratories or circles of advisers. At its most aggressive, this attitude does not merely mean a desire by industry to work in conjunction with the universities; it extends to a desire to change the way universities themselves operate, to make them resemble industrial organisations in both their internal structures and in their attitudes to work. This approach reflects an impatience with the "waste" that is necessarily involved in notions of academic freedom and the absence of hierarchical direction.

Industry may also regard the university as a competitor, since an increasing number of intelligent graduates refuse to enter industrial employment and seek to continue doing research at university. Even though this often merely means that industry will eventually be able to employ a better qualified man when his research is completed, industry is disturbed at the trend. It is interesting to see how industry is prepared to suspend its opposition to state intervention in order to seek limitation on the number of research students.

Eric Robinson uses as part of his evidence in attacking "academic" education the views of industrialists who say that such an education is unsuitable for their own purposes, but he seeks to escape the charge of narrow vocationalism by insisting that the qualities which industry deplores as lacking in such education are the same qualities as those needed for "life" in the modern world; in other words, for a proper "liberal" education. Indeed, many industrial leaders would assert that their needs are for such critical individuals as Robinson seeks to be created by a good educational system. He would differ from the "needs of industry" approach to education only if the latter implies a rigid and narrow vocationalism.

If Robinson's formula is accepted, problems continue to arise. Even if one accepts his view of the sterility of "academic" education one can still foresee that once vocational interests have been welcomed into the system it will not be sufficient to rely on a co-incidence of educational virtue and industry's desires to avoid the potential narrowness of vocationalism.

POLITICS AND THE PROBLEM OF THE UNIVERSITIES

It is now time to bring together the strands of this characterisation of differing attitudes to educational involvement with the outside world and to examine the cross-cutting nature of the educational debate where conventional political barriers are concerned.

Conservatives are to be found on the side of both isolationists and interventionists, because while on the one hand high culture belongs to them, they are also the supporters of the industrial interest and, generally speaking, the opponents of generous provision in the public services. The dilemma is usually resolved within conservative thinking by advocacy of two-tiered systems. On the one hand they seek an exclusive reservoir of high culture untroubled by baser utilitarian criteria (public schools, Oxbridge); while on the other hand they envisage a vocational system for the rest (secondary and technical schools, colleges of technology). In the current debate on government intervention in education, conservatives are likely to commend the co-existence of two systems, one as a reservoir for free academic inquiry, the other as a vocational training ground for other people's children.

Liberals and democratic radicals have no less a problem of divided aims. On the one hand is the respect held by people on the left for the tradition of critical dissent that has been able to flourish in British universities. Even if prevailing academic traditions have often been conservative, radicals have had their own traditions, and even Marxists have had an easier passage from university administrators than they have from, say, British trade-union leaders. Among students the contempt for the university which is now being shown on the far left is a new phenomenon. Marxists of earlier generations believed in the kind of knowledge they could gain from a university. The theory of the total contamination and confinement of bourgeois culture had not been developed. There is, further, a long and naïve tradition on the British left that sees education as a necessary gateway to socialism. Sidney Webb, for example, considered that conversion to socialism would be a virtually automatic consequence of an education at the LSE (which he founded).

In these ways the British left has, through its intellectual wing, been integrated into the consensus of élite culture, while in turn having a significant impact on that culture. It is here that a conflict appears between the largely middle-class intelligentsia and those technocratic populists who have at least an equal claim to be the mainstream of British radicalism. Academic radicals may well look with foreboding on the encroachments of vocationalism on to their preserve of freedom; but it is the vocational prospects of higher and further education which have attracted the attention of the working classes whose interests they are concerned to advance. It is the chance of good career opportunities for their children that provides almost the only appeal of higher education for working-class parents. It is noteworthy that, while working-class students are grossly under-represented in traditional academic institutions, they are found in much larger proportions in the technological universities and the colleges of technology. Furthermore, it is in precisely these institutions, where the sons of the working classes are prepared for lesser careers in capitalist enterprises, that student revolt has been almost entirely absent in Britain.

Alongside this preference for vocationally oriented education, there is, among the British left, a strong element of distrust of the élite academic institutions. Universities are seen very much as part of the class structure that enables the children of the existing élite to pass from public school through university and on to the same high-status positions as their parents held. From this comes the unrest among technologists and others who have not been educated in the élite traditions and who for that reason feel excluded by nepotism and an élite culture from the leading positions in industry for which they feel qualified. It was this concept of radicalism and change, and this particular image of what constituted the conservative enemy, which played so large a part in the reshaping of the Labour Party between 1959 and 1964. The Party attempted to appear as a spearhead of what were seen as new groups of politically dissatisfied professionals and technologists.

The ways in which the political parties resolve their problems of approach to higher education may in practice be very similar, even though to a certain extent they will be impelled by different motives. It is unlikely that any British government would be strong or determined enough to gnaw away at the pinnacles of academic freedom. However, it would be a logical development of current policy to try to achieve greater central direction. When Mr Crosland, as Secretary of State for Education and Science, announced the binary policy[21] he made it clear that the Government was determined to fill a need for "vocational, professional and industrially based courses" which could not be met by the universities. There was also a need for a section of higher education to be "under social control".

It is thus likely that future expansion will be concentrated in the colleges of technology, where expansion has the further attraction of being cheaper. However, we can probably also expect to see an attempt at achieving more "social control" over the university sector itself. The UGC has already changed its role from being a "buffer" between the state and the the universities to becoming, increasingly, a central co-ordinator of government policy. The next step could well be the establishment of a new body of state interference, as foreshadowed in the report of the Select Committee on Higher Education.[22]

In these conditions it becomes important that those involved in higher education think fundamentally about the direction in which events are moving, and establish to their own satisfaction where the line should be drawn between reasonable co-operation and dangerous interference. Unfortunately there is evidence that universities and their staffs will become more angered by government pressures to improve their general effectiveness and use of resources in minor administrative ways which do not affect the nature of their work.

NEW LEFT AND OLD LEFT

Into this unsettled position in higher education has emerged the student movement. We have already seen how it, like other political groupings, has a paradoxical set of attitudes towards the university question. Student revolutionaries are likely, to a limited extent, to find common cause with conservative defenders of academic privilege against the incursions of the industrial state. It is pleasantly ironic to hear such men as Hoch and Schoenbach (who feel they are so far to the left that they can denounce the LSE Marxists as moderates) speaking of the dangers of "creeping nationalisation" of the universities.[23] It is even more so to see them quoting, with apparent approval, Sir Douglas Logan,* Principal of the University of London,[24] opposing the inspection of his accounts by the Comptroller and Auditor General.†

Admittedly, their main point is not to defend academic autonomy. Rebels as estranged as Hoch and Schoenbach have only one main concern: the preservation of their own movement. For them the most important problem seems to be that, because of universities' attempts to maintain good relations with their pay-masters, they have to crack down on student revolt. However, behind the whole argument there is the implicit assumption that autonomous universities were more satisfactory than whatever is likely to emerge from a programme of state intervention.

More explicit is a discussion of these questions by David Adelstein, who has drawn attention to the fact that Robbins based his proposal for educational expansion on student demand for places. Again we may enjoy the irony of one of the LSE's leading radicals supporting the chairman of the School's Court of Governors in opposition to the policy of a Labour Government:

"In this sense the Robbins Report was 'student oriented' – it catered for apparent student demand. In so far as it based its case on the inherent value of expansion rather than upon economic demands, the Report represents possibly

* Hoch and Logan clashed several times during the LSE occupation of the ULU building (see pages 87, 90), and at one stage Logan tried to make Hoch personally responsible for damage done to the building. They clashed again in November 1969, when Hoch led an attack on the Senate House to protest at the University's links with University College, Rhodesia.

† But perhaps one should not assume too much consistency among the left. The Oxford branch of the RSSF held a protest against All Souls College to call, *inter alia*, for the public inspection of the college's accounts.

the last 'liberal' document that a government commission will produce for some time. Indeed, Robbins as an educationalist is very much a liberal heir to Newman."[25]

This support for Robbins is limited: Adelstein objects to the élitism and the latent traditionalism of Robbins's approach, but he proceeds with a criticism of the Labour Government's treatment of the Robbins proposals which on the whole takes Robbins as a positive point of reference. As we have observed before, the irony of this position is an indication of the gulf which has appeared between the new left and the centralising technocratic left represented in the Labour Party. To the latter the idea of bringing education into a closer relationship with career preparation is egalitarian and democratic; to such a man as Adelstein it is anathema. The difference is precisely that between a party which seeks to pursue its aims of democratic reform through the existing institutions of the society and a group which regards those very institutions with a deep suspicion and fear.

One should acknowledge that Adelstein's view of the Robbins Report, or at least certain sections of it, is more accommodating than other commentaries from the far left. A pamphlet published by International Socialism,[26] most of the authors of which were prominent LSE revolutionaries, describes the Robbins Report as the "first systematic attempt to relate the structure of higher education to the needs of a modernised capitalism". Robbins's desire for criteria other than the economic to govern university policy is acknowledged, but is generally regarded as an archaic determination to maintain an élite culture. Academic freedom is described as "immensely valuable", but is regarded as far too limited to be of any use to the revolution.[27] Where the major direction of policy is concerned, the universities are seen as being very directly subject to the dictates of the capitalist class, whether through government power or through the heavy representation of that class on universities' supreme governing bodies. Educational documents making mention of a relationship between the work of universities and wider criteria are quoted, with words like "industry" and "in the light of national needs" being picked out in angry bold letters.[28, 29]

However, it is of significance that although the language and mood are revolutionary and of the left there is much in the horror expressed at the idea of industry and commerce that reminds one of an earlier aristocratic disdain for contamination by trade and industrial grime. There is also something of the sense of holiness attached to education; the money-changers are to be driven from the temple.

The revolutionary's dilemma over this attitude to the traditional university has been neatly captured by David Martin in the course of an analogy between the traditional university and the monastery; the radical students rebuke the monks for refusing to enter the world and its troubles. But their attitude is more ambiguous than this:

"The paradox can be illustrated by one young sociologist who said he had no intention of becoming a junior manager . . . he had a fundamental objection to being incarcerated in a restrictive secular role with no 'spiritual' returns consonant with his horizons. Of course he also objected to the monastic concept of the university. Yet without the catholic perspectives of a university, and the ecumenical sweep of sociology, he could never have found the language of protest. . . .
"Most reformers are like Martin Luther: ex-monks. They strive not only to reform but to destroy institutions without which they could not have come into existence."[30]

CONCLUSION

We have now surveyed some of the main approaches to the problematic relation of the university to the world and have tried to set the approach of the new left into this context. Three factors of major importance to a full understanding of the character of the new left and why it exists as a force within our universities have emerged from this study. To summarise: first, there is a deep-rooted belief that the power of economic institutions and the interdependence of institutions in a modern polity have rendered the universities yet another instrument of the ruling class, yet another element in the control exercised over our lives by the depersonalising forces of monopoly capitalism and the bourgeois state.

It has been noted that whereas Marx took as his model of man in society the conditions of Victorian sweated industry the new left have as their model man working in modern mass-production industry. The university is part of the mass-production system. It is co-ordinated with and feeds into the economic system in its educational activities, and its research is also carefully programmed to the needs of industry. The university and its vaunted freedoms are a myth, a mystification by the bourgeois capitalist class to divert attention from the truth. From this position it is a short step to the view that all education, and not simply the more obviously vocational aspects, are part of a bourgeois mystification. The university therefore requires to be exposed, its true nature to be laid bare. One of the functions of student revolt is to carry out this task of stripping naked, and a few student protests have had this precise task (e.g. at Essex – the germ warfare case – and at Glasgow). The university protest is also seen in this way as just one aspect of a wider problem that exists throughout society. The internal conflicts and the wider concerns of the student revolutionaries meet at this crucial point.

Second, of particular importance in the conflict of approaches to the relationship of the universities to the world is the divergence between the view of the revolutionaries and that of the orthodox Labour movement, and in particular that of the Labour Government. This is related to the former point and intensifies the strength of alienation from conventional political channels felt by the new left. This will be taken up in further detail in the following chapter.

Finally, the students' ideal image of the university and their love-hate relationship with existing institutions indicates some important characteristics of this revolt. The university is expected to be different from other institutions. Industry, the army, the church, the civil service, are all obviously institutions in which the new left has no faith at all; the university, however, has pretensions to something different. Many young leftists are the children of radical parents of a previous university generation; as we have noted before, the student revolt is as much a revolt against an earlier liberalism as it is against more traditional foes of the left. The universities represent, in some of their traditions, the philosophy of that liberalism; rational debate, intelligent concern, scepticism, a certain type of withdrawal from industry and commerce. It is these values that are now being condemned as inadequate and hypocritical. We are now ready to leave discussion of the university and examine this wider political context in closer detail.

REFERENCES

1. Report of Committee on Higher Education (Robbins), 1963, Cmnd 2154
2. Independent projections by the Department of Education and Science, and by the Higher Education Research Unit, London School of Economics, November 1969
3. Robbins, *op cit*, Ch II
4. *ibid*, Ch XI
5. Particularly as outlined in speeches by Mr A. Crosland, when Secretary of State for Education and Science, at Woolwich Polytechnic (April 27 1965) and at the University of Lancaster (January 20 1967)
6. Council for Scientific Policy, *Enquiry into the Flow of Candidates in Science and Technology into Higher Education*, 1968, Cmnd 3541
7. For a discussion of the trend in policy on this issue, see Layard, R. and King, J., "Expansion Since Robbins" (in Martin, D. (ed), *Anarchy and Culture*, 1969)
8. Ford, B., "What Is a University?", (*New Statesman*, October 24 1969)
9. *Universities Quarterly*, Spring 1969
10. Halsey, A. H., "The Universities and the State" (*ibid*, p 138)
11. *ibid*, p 137

12. Ashby, E., ". . . *And Scholars*", 1964, p 18
13. Robbins, *op cit*, p 6
14. Halliday, F., "Students of the World Unite" (in Cockburn, A. and Blackburn, R. (eds), *Student Power*, 1969, p 299)
15. Marx, K., *Theses on Feuerbach*
16. Some interesting arguments on a related theme can be found in Gellner, E., "The Panther and the Dove" (in Martin, *op cit*)
17. Crosland, A., *The Conservative Enemy*, 1962, Ch II
18. Robinson, E., *The New Polytechnics*, 1968
19. *ibid*, p 91
20. Kerr, C., *The Uses of the University*, 1963. Kerr has related student revolt to his ideas in "The New Involvement with Society" (*Dialogue*, Vol 1 No 1)
21. Crosland, Woolwich speech, *op cit*
22. Report from Select Committee on Education and Science, 1969, pp 55, 56
23. Hoch, P. and Schoenbach, V., *LSE: The Natives Are Restless*, 1969, p 167
24. Logan, D., *Calendar 1968–9*, University of London
25. Adelstein, D., "Roots of the British Crisis" (in Cockburn and Blackburn, *op cit*, p 65)
26. Harman, C., et alii, *Education, Capitalism and the Student Revolt*, International Socialism, 1968, p 26
27. *ibid*, p 14
28. *ibid*, pp 11, 25f
29. See also Newman, J., "Education and Politics in Britain" (in Nagel, J. (ed), *Student Power*, 1969)
30. Martin, D., "The Dissolution of the Monasteries" (in Martin, *op cit*, p 4)

PART THREE

*Student Revolt
and British Politics*

CHAPTER EIGHT

Student Revolt and British Politics

We began by briefly setting the new left in a context of
wider politics, before going on to burrow more deeply into
the narrower area where it has performed its most important
activities to date: the universities. With the discussion in the
previous chapter of the university and the world we have
come full circle and can see again the new left in terms of its
reaction to certain wider political developments. We must
now look at some of the major changes which have affected
British society and politics in the past few years and which
are of relevance to the development of student dissent.

Inevitably, the pace and level of the discussion must now
change. We have devoted close attention to the minutiae of
student revolts, but we must now move swiftly and cursorily
through far more important political and philosophical issues.
But the imbalance is inevitable. To neglect discussion of
these wider themes would be to leave out of consideration
factors which are relevant to our theme; on the other hand,
to cover them with the same detail that we have devoted to
student revolt would require several books and several major
research projects. We must be content with a brief survey of
a wide field. If the previous chapters have tried to achieve a
degree of comprehensiveness, here we are trying to be provocative of new thought and further discussion.

In Chapters Five and Six in particular we have tried to
explain what is implied by the novel forms of organisation
and action which have been developing within the student
movement. We have concentrated on the movement in Britain, but these categories are of more general application and
may in fact be even more relevant to an understanding of the

movements in West Germany and the USA. These characteristics are those which distinguish the student movement
from more familiar left-wing groupings of the recent past and
which cause considerable disquiet to others on the left, particularly perhaps the old-school Marxists.

The student movement becomes more readily understandable if we see it, not in terms of conventional political groupings, but as a particular type of social movement which has
been encountered before, often in a religious context. Its
appearance can be related to certain features of prevailing
forms of social organisation; it is very much a reactive phenomenon and can only be appreciated as a set of articulated
contrasts with such prevailing forms.

We have tried to suggest in previous chapters how this
pattern of contrasts operates within the university. In this
chapter we shift from this local level to one of broad generality. We then relate the particular response of the student
movement, first to certain broad themes about the development of socialism, bureaucracy and technology, and finally
to certain events in very recent history in this country.

In discussion of the revolt against authority in the university we saw how in the course of a protest the movement
developed a model of authority which countered at every
point that of bureaucratic forms. We no longer need restrict
our model to the internal university situation. On a general
level, bureaucracy stresses rigidity of structure; the new left
seeks free forms of organisation. It implies the division of
labour; the new left condemns the division of labour as
alienation. Bureaucracy sees participation in terms of formal
representative and nominative structures; the new left seeks
the total egalitarian experience of mass participation. It
works through roles and secondary relations; its adherents
believe in primary, face-to-face relations. Bureaucracy operates according to formal rules and tries to achieve freedom
from value decisions; they seek an existentialist morality
where ultimate ethical choices confront a man in his every
action.

It is this last point above all which characterises the new

left's disgust with impersonal formal bureaucracy and which relates their counter-authority to the charismatic. It is also this point which most clearly relates one of the critiques of the university to a critique of the wider political system.

It appears to the student radical that modern politics constantly avoids questions of moral choice through appeal to the logic of bureaucratic rationality. Similarly, a massive state apparatus has been erected against the puny attempts of the individual man, or groups of men, to follow their objectives and develop as free human beings. It is characteristic of charisma that it should emerge in political or religious situations where the ethical point of reference has been squeezed to the margin, where change through smoother and more constitutional procedures appears to be no longer available, and where tradition and rationality are not respected sufficiently to enable them to guide or channel thought and action. There is a desire to burst through the confines of the mundane, to reach out to ultimate values and to seek a transformation in human experience.

THE REVOLT AGAINST REASON

In Chapter Five we suggested that the demand for "community" so often expressed by the student radicals did not mean at all a desire for community as traditionally conceived, but for a type of social relationship that parallels the charismatic. Here again we meet with points of a wider reference. An extremely similar model of action was suggested in a little-known essay by the German sociologist Schmalenbach,[1] who places the kind of structure we saw being developed in a primitive way in the university into a far more universal context.

His starting point is, rightly, the difference between communal ties rooted in tradition and those rooted in effect. Schmalenbach calls his model the "Bund" and his translators render this quite satisfactorily as "communion". The concept is applied to that attempt to seek a continuity of immediate experience unmediated by structures, forms and routine. A valuable example of this urge that is suggested by

Schmalenbach is the often expressed resentment when "love" becomes routinised as "faithfulness" in the course of marriage. There is disquiet and suspicion of all routines that detract from the depth and passion of immediate sentiments.

Duverger[2] has discussed Schmalenbach's concept in the context of political organisations of a certain type, and the student radicals easily fit into this category. But Schmalenbach also applies it to religious groups – to the important distinction between the church and the sect. The sect is here seen as an attempt to oppose the institutionalisation of religion (the church) and to renew the immediacy of religious experience. As with charisma, the attempt is doomed to failure because of the essential transitoriness of the depth of passion that these attempts seek to create. In certain of its features the student dissent resembles the sect, even to the extent that it parallels the distinction, often found among Protestant sects, between the practical, even revolutionary, and the withdrawn and quietist.

There are yet more important similarities between the themes of the student revolt and those of modern theologians.[3] Just as the theologian sees God as the "Ground of our Being", so the new Marxist is concerned that men should be able to live according to their fundamental "species-life". Where the theologian is concerned at the constraints imposed on the pure expression of the spirit by the formal structures and ordinances of the Church, so the new left is impatient with the structures and constraints imposed by "class society". Spontaneity is the crucial value to both the theologian who believes he should celebrate the Eucharist anywhere, perhaps in the street, and to the revolutionary who elevates the spontaneous experience of the mass to a place at the peak of human action. Some elements in contemporary theology are seeking a role for the religious as non-institutional, non-structured, deliberately set as a contrast to the mundane and the organised. Here again there are similarities in the definition of socialism which is appearing on the new left.

To a certain extent, of course, we are comparing movements which have a common range of ancestors, through Kirkegaard and others, in existentialism. In this study we are not concerned to explain student revolt by delineating its intellectual mentors, because such an explanation simply relocates the question and we have to ask why certain writers should be more influential than others. Our present interest is a more direct one; we need to understand the student revolt as a response to certain characteristics of social and political organisation. In this we encounter several other contemporary movements which are articulating similar attitudes and philosophies. One of them is the new theology; another which would reward attention is modern art.

In modern art there is a strong resistance to structure and form, which in an earlier generation were considered the essence of art. Now the emphasis is on spontaneity, on opposition to structure, on the psychedelic (which attempts to reach a "reality" beyond the allegedly distorted perceptions of the structured senses). There is also an obsession with *objets trouvés*, and in music composers try to develop free forms of composition, ignoring the structures of musical notation and frequently leaving it to the discretion of the performer in which order he plays the different sections of a piece.

The different attitudes of the 18th and mid-20th centuries towards art and nature are paralleled by the change in philosophical approaches to reason and passion. The 18th century saw art as man's triumph over nature, asserting a noble order over chaos, and reason as the author of man's liberation from the slavery of the unmediated senses and emotions. The modern tends to reject art as artifice and sees rationality as slavery. At the same time, with the demise of reason, art finds a new rationale for an engagement in politics.[4] The new left has had little effect on the main outline of political structure in our society, but its related influence in the arts, pop culture and fashion has been powerful, and often the left assert their revolutionary life style and cultural mores as part of their protest; this is part of the essence of cultural revolution.[5]

The "revolt against reason" is central to the whole process. Richard Lowenthal[6] has traced the developments within the Marxist theory of revolution which led away from Marx's own formulation of revolution depending on the rational resolution of certain laws of historical development. In the face of the refractory course of subsequent history there has grown up an alternative, indeed opposed, concept of action which creates its own logic and then imposes itself on subsequent developments. This sets a theory of extreme voluntarism against the Marxist determinism, but it is a consistent development of existentialism, with its reversal of the rationalist's sequence of action following premeditation and calculation. It is also consistent with the ideas of resentment at an imposed situational logic and institutional constraint which we have discussed above. The idea that one should try to alter the rigidities of a surrounding structure by dramatic innovatory activity can be entirely rational and sound political sense. However, when adopted as a policy of conscious opposition to notions of calculation it has the practical effect of making a virtue of irrationalism. There is a kind of democratisation of charisma; every man becomes his own radical innovator.

It is not difficult to relate these developments to contemporary problems of politics; some of the major elements were outlined in Chapter One. Rationality appears to the young radical in the form of rationalisation, of bureaucratisation, and as an instrument for controlling and manipulating other human beings. It is Karl Mannheim's[7] distinction between substantive and functional rationality. It also goes back to the nemesis of rationalism that obsessed Max Weber, seeing reason the liberator become reason the enslaver through its embodiment in organisational bureaucracy. In previous chapters we have found elements of Weber's discussion of authority and organisation useful in analysing our material. Although many different historical studies lie behind the formulation of Weber's concepts, they were in many ways related to the political crisis of his own time, and it is no coincidence that Weber showed considerable interest in student movements of his time which were concerned with the apparent deterioration in the "meaningfulness" of life with the growth of the Prussian bureaucracy and certain features of economic development. Weber sympathised with their concern, though he could not follow them in their pursuit of absolute ethical certainty.[8]

It is to similar themes that contemporary students try to relate themselves. It would be an interesting task to tackle the question of the extent to which there has been a decline in "meaningfulness", to what extent modern social organisation deprives man of individuality at a time when he seems to have more individual freedom than at any other. But to attempt to deal with this is obviously beyond our study, and in some ways it does not matter whether it is objectively true or not. An important point is that many young people on the left seem to think it is true, and interpret certain political developments as indicating its truth. All we can do here is to consider some of these developments which appear relevant in the formation of these attitudes in a particular sphere.

Since we are concerned with British left-wing students who have come to believe in the impossibility of orthodox politics and in the malevolence of state institutions, it is particularly relevant to take as an object of study the contemporary British Labour Party. Certain trends in the party's recent development, reflecting the wider changes in the economy and social structure, reveal tensions between socialism and rationalism, between central power and local interests, and between the state as controller and the state as servant of powerful social interests. It is from these tensions that the new left has derived certain of its stances. No doubt study of change in other relevant institutions could suggest similar influences.

SOCIALISM AND RATIONALISM

To a large extent the objectives of socialist politics and those of rationalisation coincide, and it seems strange to set the two in opposition to one another. Both concepts imply an attack on unjustified privilege and on prejudice, and both involve principles of universalism and equality. Both are scornful of tradition. Both seek to assert human control and the planning of social life. They tend to differ in the relation to ultimate objectives; a policy of "rationalisation" alone cannot provide the ends of policy; these have to be prescribed from outside the rational model. Thus if politicians see themselves principally as rationalisers they may neglect problems of the objectives of policy and simply concern themselves with the most efficient means of achieving ends which are largely given to them by the existing political and social structure.

Given the inequalities in the ability of different interest groups to impose their own priorities on the political system as a whole, a policy of simple rationalisation is likely to reflect these biases. There are therefore various ways in which a policy of rationalisation may clash with egalitarian aspirations if these latter are not given determined attention.

The interests of rationalisation and those of a labour movement can clash in a different way. Rationalisation always implies change; socialism tends to imply change. This fact obscures the tension which may exist between the two and provides a further instance of the dangers of equating them. Social change has so often been a slogan of the left that it has frequently escaped attention that change can just as easily involve disruption of the interests sponsored by the left as it can promote them. This has become especially true in such a society as our own where labour organisations are deeply entrenched and where ordinary people have acquired a firm network of rights and benefits.

Many of the arguments in favour of economic rationalisation involve severe threats to these rights, as can be seen from an examination of current policies for change in the position of trade unions and for selectivity in the social services. There can be no *a priori* assumption that greater formal justice and change in the direction of ironing out anomalies will work to the interest of the under-privileged. It is often the case that anomalies and settled practices protect the interests of relatively under-privileged groups and that the introduction of greater rationality and universality, far from assisting them, simply entrenches the position of the privileged in the society as a whole.

226

These problems have been thrown into a new and more urgent focus by the emergence of the modern technological economy. Modern technology demands, not the sharp winds of free competition, but a stable social environment, in which governments play their part in economic planning, restrictive legislation and rationalisation. So far our knowledge of these processes is rudimentary, but an attempt has been made to analyse them by J. K. Galbraith[9] and the results of his analysis lead to conclusions about the development of contemporary politics consistent with those we have already outlined.

Although this problem has been studied by Galbraith with particular reference to the USA, the questions are becoming more generally applicable. He argues that six major trends in technological development are responsible:

First, an increasing span of time separates the beginning from the completion of any task.

Second, there is an increase in the capital that is committed to production aside from that occasioned by increased output.

Third, the commitment of time and money tends to be made ever more inflexibly to the performance of a particular task.

Fourth, technology requires specialised manpower.

Fifth, concomitant with specialisation is an extremely complex organisation.

Finally, from the time and capital that must be committed, the inflexibility of this commitment, the needs of large organisation and the problems of market performance under conditions of advanced technology, comes the necessity for planning.

The irony of this development, fully appreciated by Galbraith, is that certain policies of state intervention in industry, which have traditionally been associated with socialism, become the needs of industry, and the objectives to be served by these policies become changed in the process.

Thus it is central to Galbraith's analysis that governments are increasingly called upon to underwrite industry's capital investment, because the risk-bearing cost is too great for a private corporation. In principle this should give government an increasing power of the purse, and to a certain extent this does occur. However, the context in which this process takes place tends increasingly to the reverse. Industry is often able to argue that if a particular project is not sponsored the industry will decline, we shall become less competitive overseas, and there will be increasing unemployment. Thus the initiative in the process lies with the industry, and its needs in a complex economy are readily identified with a national interest.

A second way in which the new industrial structure impinges on government prerogatives is that the state is called upon to assist industry in securing and co-ordinating its resources and in carrying out its plans. Third, government has to play a role in ensuring the stability of markets that is desired by industry; incomes policies and industrial relations policies are important instances of this. Fourth, there is a new need for concentration in industry in order to achieve the scale required for modern technology. The clearest expression of this new role for government in helping industry to become yet bigger and more powerful in Britain is the Industrial Reorganisation Corporation.

Finally, constraints are imposed on government action by the growth of the international corporation. A firm which has its operations within the confines of one nation state must to a high degree be subject to the decisions of government on such matters as location. If, however, a firm can pick and choose between different countries, it is able to select areas where restrictions imposed on its activities are least and thereby exert an influence against restrictions in various countries. This again furthers the power of the industrial interest.

A proper study of the relationship between industry and government in an advanced economy would obviously be able to present a far more thorough, rigorous and balanced account than this anecdotal discussion. But it suffices for present purposes if we can deduce from what has been discussed certain broad political trends. The major points would seem to be that, as a result of changes in the industrial structure, there is a new industrial dependence on and influence over government policy and the direction of government involvement in industry. The rhetoric of socialism becomes translated into the politics of industrial rationalisation. As a result of this the political process becomes one of administration, and conflicts of interest are minimised. When the objective of politics is simply an efficient economy, and when the dynamic of reaching political objectives is seen in terms of increasing technology, the only relevant conflict of interest becomes the modernisers versus those standing in the way of change.

We are now able to examine how these issues have come together in the period of Labour Government in Britain 1964–1970. Unfortunately, our discussion can only be anecdotal and hint at one or two events or observed trends.

CHANGE IN THE LABOUR PARTY

A watershed in the development of recent British politics was the general election of 1959, when the Labour Party suffered its third successive defeat in a general election, and by a large majority. In the mood of introspection and self-recrimination that followed, both right and left wings of the party produced their analysis of failure and their prescriptions for recovery and success. The left sought to restore a perspective of class consciousness and an onslaught on private ownership, to go out and win back the mass of working people from the embrace of an inegalitarian and allegedly soulless affluence to an identification with the policies of socialism.

The Labour right, on the other hand, concluded from the changing social structure of Britain a need for Labour to change direction away from these concerns of the left. Whatever the vicissitudes of the different factions in terms of policy decisions at conferences and elections for the leadership, it is now clear that this second faction, or rather its viewpoint, eventually came to dominate the party. Indeed the roots of its victory can be detected even before the actual débâcle of

1959. From early in the 1950s, and particularly after the accession of Hugh Gaitskell to the party leadership, the revisionists had been at work. Anthony Crosland's extremely influential *The Future of Socialism* appeared in 1956.

Perhaps the most important of the changes in social structure to which the factions were responding was the effect on social class of the gradual increase in affluence that had been taking place, especially since 1945. Social and economic inequalities were being pushed back so that they were operating in less stark and crucial areas of life than in, say, the 1920s and 1930s. Although in reality the structure of inequality remained substantially the same, this shift lessened the salience of many class differentials, and gave the impression to many that class no longer existed.[10] The Labour Party as a whole, as opposed to groups within it, had never been an aggressively class-conscious party; it had always tried to represent the cause of the working man in terms of rights gained through the British constitution, which meant, in practice, accepting major elements of the social structure of the country. However, the party's rhetoric and policies had been based on the manual working class as an under-privileged group, and the advancement of the socialist cause was seen to lie in the public ownership of a wide range of industries, relieving of their power the capitalist owning class, and in the radical shift of investment, through state power, from private to publicly owned social development.

With the changes in class structure this appeal seemed less relevant. The working class lacked the self-consciousness that such a view implied, and several sections of that class were doing reasonably well within the structure of a privately-owned economy. Further, there were signs that the manual working class was undergoing long-term numerical decline, as old industries died and new industries with a different occupational structure emerged. There was growing interest within the higher reaches of the party in ways in which they could attract the votes of the rising new middle classes.[11]

Parallel with this development there was a general disillusion with public ownership, a major element in Labour's identity as a party. There was little public enthusiasm for such a policy, and there was precious little evidence that public ownership had in fact done anything to change the social structure in the way that had been hoped by early idealists. The capitalist class did not appear to have been dispossessed, and, with the possible exception of the coal industry, nationalisation did not seem to have any effect on internal industrial relations. It mattered little whether an employer was a private firm or a state concern.

An additional disadvantage of nationalisation which weighed heavily on such men as Hugh Gaitskell was the danger of the emergence of huge state monopolies as had been witnessed in Eastern Europe and the USSR. Also, the view was becoming current that in any case the ownership of industry was of little consequence in the modern economy, as control had passed from the capitalist to his powerful employee-managers; in this the nationalised industries were very similar to the private sector. Not only was the managerial revolution regarded as having wrought real changes in the structure of industrial control but it was also considered by Crosland[12] and others to represent a change in the direction of more intelligent and humane management and industrial relations.

If class differentials were ceasing to be important, and if the ownership of industry was becoming increasingly irrelevant to politics, why did those taking this view consider there was a continuing need for radicalism in politics? Why not support the modern Conservative Party, which had supervised the development of the affluent society and was not encumbered with what were now being considered as outmoded concepts of class and industrial power? Here the Labour right found an important and valuable expression of their views in the writing of J. K. Galbraith, and his distinction between private affluence and public squalor.[13]

Translated into terms of British politics, the argument ran thus: we can rely on the progress of the economy for a rise in the prosperity of the people, and the old distinctions of class are less important. Political debate now centres on the way in which the increasing wealth is to be spent; should it go towards increased private consumption, which will tend to benefit the better off, or should it be channelled into the public services, where it will be spent on social provision for the relatively poor, leading to a fairer, juster, more egalitarian society? The Labour right came down firmly in favour of a constantly increasing share of natural resources being devoted to the public social services. This policy was to distinguish a Labour approach from a Conservative one, both in the emphasis on the public sector and in the egalitarianism.[14]

Although these thinkers were able in this way to locate themselves within important strands of mainstream Labour tradition, their criticism of other elements of this tradition made them something of an out-group. The final transformation of Labour's orientation from a class-conscious manual workers' party to a party seeking to secure a place among the rising new elements in the occupational and social structure, while maintaining its commitment to social justice, had to await the arrival of Harold Wilson in the party leadership. To use an analogy similar to that which Wilson himself has adopted, Gaitskell had tried, in his attempted amendment of Clause Four of the Party's constitution, to change the wording of the Creed. Wilson, in consummately English fashion, achieved a gradual reinterpretation of it. He was greatly assisted in this process by the decline into chronic economic difficulty that Britain was encountering from the early sixties onward.

This decline was in fact of far older vintage, and had been important ever since Britain began to lose its place as a leading industrial innovator. The countries which industrialised after Britain did so with the ability to take advantage of Britain's experience; therefore it gradually came about that Britain, far from being the innovator, was now lagging behind in the quality of plant, equipment, processes and techniques. International economic crises in the 1920s and 1930s, and two world wars, prevented this problem from coming to the forefront until this relatively calm period of the early sixties. Meanwhile, with the loss of Empire and the decline of Britain's role in the world dramatised by the Suez episode, the security of Britain's overall position became open to question and the self-assurance of the conduct of national affairs began to stumble.

The way was open for an attack on the traditional ruling élite of the society, not necessarily because it was undemocratic or unjust, but because it was inefficient. There was scope for a call for reform in the management of industry, not because of policies of workers' control and egalitarianism but because management had grown settled in its ways and was resting on its privileges and past laurels. This was the course on which Harold Wilson and his colleagues embarked, and it was achieved by re-interpreting traditional socialist concerns in the terms of this essentially technical and managerial critique.[15] The traditional socialist concern for attacking privilege by attacking the ruling class on behalf of the masses became translated into an attack on nepotism and inefficiency on behalf of the meritocracy and the innovators. The traditional socialist concern for nationalisation as the disinheritance of the ruling class became translated as public ownership in the interests of greater efficiency and rationalisation.

A similar process took place in socialist policies for planning. It was becoming increasingly apparent even to the Conservative Party that the management of a large modern economy required a good deal of planning, co-ordinated at central government level. In Europe the Commission of the Common Market had been carrying out such activities since the Treaty of Rome without it being considered an instrument of aggressive socialism. This development was related to the decline of the market economy consequent on the emergence of large firms and complex products that could not be made subject to the normal free-market regulators. In Britain the Conservative Party had been slow and reluctant to accept such measures because they seemed to smack of socialism, whereas Labour had a well entrenched ideology of centralisation, rational planning and state intervention. Labour thus moved into a mood of confidence and assurance

233

in the debates over economic planning, incomes policy, regional development and so forth that pre-occupied national politics from 1962 onwards. In contrast, the Conservative Party went through agonies of conscience and lost its nerve. No one in the Labour Party appears to have noticed at the time that the socialist intentions of democratisation and so forth were gradually disappearing from the ways in which these policies were articulated.

Of course, in part the clash between the reformulated policies and the old slogans was not so stark. There were two reasons for this. First, one of the major avowed intentions of the new stress on efficiency was the greater wealth of Britain, and hence a higher standard of living for its people. This seemed quite consonant with the aims of the left. Second, the picture presented here of the change wrought by Wilson and his colleagues is an exaggerated one. The tendency for social-ist concerns to be translated in practice into politically neutral rational efficiency is well entrenched in Labour's history.[16] What was novel in the period from 1962 onwards was the explicit enunciation of this policy and its primary position in the image Labour desired to present:

"For what we offer is an exciting programme calling forth all the finest qualities of our people: their energy, their skill, their tenacity, and their spirit of adventure. We must put behind us the idea that the world owes us a living and that we can muddle on in an amateurish way. Our prob-lem of getting off the ground, of overcoming the forces of inertia, is a problem familiar to the pioneers of space travel. We must develop more thrust. The Tory Party, by its very nature, is incapable of providing this thrust. A Labour Government will provide it. That is how we shall build our new Britain together."[17]

The policy achieved one of its major objectives in that it paved the way for Labour to appeal as the party to which the rising generations of technical and scientific workers could look to represent their interests. At the same time it enabled Labour, in the prolonged election campaign of

1963–64, to stake its position squarely in the area of widespread concern: Britain's economic stability and confidence in its continually increasing prosperity.

In 1964 the Labour Party had achieved a concise reformulation of its traditional doctrines that appeared to be well attuned to the major political issues of the times. How did this reformation fare in practice in certain key events in the life of the Labour Government?

In the summer of 1966 the Prime Minister appeared on television to attack the strike of the National Union of Seamen. A group of under-privileged and ill-paid workers were, through their official trade union, seeking to put pressure on their powerful employers. And a Labour Prime Minister took steps to condemn them nationally and to hint at a whole host of sinister motives in their activity. Many people in the Labour Party were shocked. This seemed at variance with what they considered to be the role and policy of the Labour Party; it was felt that in some way the party had changed, or that the Government was acting contrary to the party's philosophy.

But exactly what had changed? The rhetoric of the 1964 and 1966 election campaigns was still there in the Prime Minister's speech. He was saying that the power of the Government and the machinery of state must be used to ensure that nothing interfere with our economic recovery. The cardinal aim of policy was to ensure success in the achievement of a balance of payments surplus, and no irrational interest groups must be allowed to intrude their private interests in the way of this overriding national goal. These were the slogans of 1964 and 1966; slogans into which many people in the Labour movement had read a determination by a Labour Government to use the state apparatus to oppose privileged groups, both traditional and capitalist, who stood in the way of the welfare and prosperity of the British people.

But it had been forgotten that the old slogans had been given a new interpretation, and in the course of this process they had inevitably changed in meaning. Such concepts as attacks on privilege and denunciation of private interests standing in the way of national goals remained, but the goals were now defined in terms of economic rationalisation and technical efficiency, not the usual concerns of the Labour movement. If one adopts this redefinition, the problem of the Labour Government's policy towards the seamen's strike disappears; far from being at variance with official policy, it was a thoroughly valid expression of it.

Second, there was the National Plan.[18] Defined in terms of socialism, the objective of a National Plan would be to secure a degree of "democratic" control over the conduct of the economy; to subject industry to the criteria of responsibility to social ends; to make possible the assertion of social priority over private economic interest. Certainly one would have expected the policy to involve a change in the balance of private affluence and public squalor.

This particular question has been considered at length by Brian Abel-Smith,[19] who begins a study of Labour's social plans with some quotations from Crosland:[20]

"Today we all accept some communal responsibility for overcoming poverty, distress and social squalor. The question is whether we do so gladly or grudgingly, and what priority we give it. A Socialist is identified as one who wishes to give this an exceptional priority over other resources. . . . This represents the first major difference between a Socialist and a Conservative. . . . The balance between public and private spending is wrong. We shall not put matters right unless we increase the proportion of the national income devoted to social purposes."

Abel-Smith then goes on to show how under the National Plan it was in fact envisaged that the gap between social and private spending would narrow less quickly than it had under the last six years of Conservative government:

". . . the public services (current) and housing increased by 34·5 per cent in constant prices between 1958 and 1964 and are planned to increase by only 28 per cent between 1964 and 1970. Thus the absolute rate of growth was greater in the six years preceding 1964 than in the six years planned from 1964 onwards.

236

"The plan provides for about the same overall rate of growth of the economy between 1964 and 1970 – of 25 per cent compared with an achieved growth of 25·4 per cent between 1959 and 1964. Whereas the plan provides for an increase of personal consumption of 21 per cent between 1958 and 1964 personal consumption actually rose in real terms by 23 per cent between 1958 and 1964. Thus Labour's plan gives more relative weight to personal consumption compared with public services and housing than the Tories during the last six years of their administration. Or to put it another way, the gap between private spending and 'social' spending narrowed faster under the Tories than under Labour's plan for the future."[21]

The objectives of the plan are surprising and unexpected if one assumes that one of Labour's basic intentions in its economic planning was the redistribution of resources from private to social spending. If, on the other hand, one accepts that the party's major planning objective was the provision of a stable environment for industry, and so forth, the policy becomes entirely understandable.

Of course, we are speaking here of the party's position where its economic planning policy was concerned; other areas of the party policy had not necessarily changed in the same direction. This becomes evident when we follow out the results of the National Plan. It received a severe set-back with the July 1966 measures, and was formally abandoned after the November 1967 devaluation. The disillusion and disaffection within the party throughout those extremely difficult months had had to be met by concessions; for a long time the social services were protected from the cuts being imposed on the private sector. In practice, the gap between private and public spending has narrowed more than had been envisaged under the plan. In other words, the usual interests of the Labour movement tended to do better in the old-fashioned politicking process, and came out badly in the first major attempt at the radical new politics of rational planning on whose slogans Labour had come to power in 1964.

A final area of policy where we can see at work certain

forces which disrupt traditional concerns of the Labour Party is that of industrial relations and incomes policy; the seamen's strike was, of course, an early instance of the policy. Obviously, there are many complex arguments on this vexed issue, but here we can single out a relatively simple aspect: the general political climate in which the debate has taken place. Strikes are seen simply in terms of their effect on industrial production. Although the overall effects of strike action on the country's economic performance are relatively slight, especially in comparison with, say, the internal activities of some international corporations, it is purely within this context that the activities of trade unions are discussed. The notion of the strike as a countervailing power against the employer seems to have disappeared. The time lost each year through strikes is but a fraction of that lost through industrial accidents, but it receives far greater political and public attention. Similarly, incomes policy was justified on the grounds that it would aid workers in poorly paid industries. There is little evidence that this was the result.[22]

To seek the rationale for attempted prohibitions on strike action and for incomes policy one probably has to look beyond the stated objectives of the policy to the wider needs of the industrial structure. The large modern corporation needs, above all, stability in order to plan and control its markets and prices and to ensure the smooth progress of work on its plant. Once again, if one views the modern Labour Party, and the network of national economic bodies it sponsored in government, as agents of technological development rather than as a party wedded to a set of social policy aims and linked to a wider labour movement, the idea of trade union legislation and incomes policy becomes readily understandable.

The above discussion has been able to do little more than clutch at straws in the wind in order to determine the nature of the changes taking place. It does however seem to be the case that the established political left in Britain, that is the Labour Party, has tended to redefine political issues in terms of technical problems, to accept narrow economic constraints on action, and to see as the only relevant area of political conflict that between modernisers and slackers. The process has by no means been completed yet; we are speaking of a discernible trend. And there is no necessary reason to assume that the trend is ineluctable; it may reach a point where Labour maintains a corner of interest for social welfare and the like.

However, the changes have been sufficiently noticeable to give concern to many radicals who would otherwise be likely to find their political home within the constitutional left. Alasdair MacIntyre[23] has succinctly summarised the observed tendency. He regards the Labour Party as having disenfranchised the working class by changing from being the party representing them to being the party representing technology.

A similar process in the decline in political life results from a different but related process. In 1964 the technological revolution was seen by Labour to represent a solution to many existing problems of economy and polity. The general idea was that increased technological growth would lead to greater prosperity, from which an increasing proportion could be devoted to the social services. Meanwhile, conservatism as the source of delay in technical progress would be opposed. The notion of a "second industrial revolution" was much vaunted, and the distinctive contribution of Labour would be to ensure that this revolution would be carried out humanely and without the callous disregard for the victims of progress which was evinced in our initial industrialisation.[24]

But the range of issues which was considered to come within the scope of this "revolution without tears" was narrowly conceived. It is only in recent years that we have come to appreciate the whole set of conflicts of interest which technological change brings in its wake. At present we are beginning to be aware of the threat posed to many interests by urban motorway development and environmental pollution. Our existing structure of political institutions seems inadequate to reflect and cope with these conflicts, and politics retreats into technical questions of administration.

A similar discussion could consider the declining scope for

initiative in overseas policy, how our structure of economic interdependence leads us to support offensive regimes and to find ourselves increasingly estranged from the starving new nations of the recently colonial world. But it is probably sufficient simply to point out that these problems exist; it is a simple matter to recognise the way in which they have affected the political perspectives of a new generation of radical youth. The economic structure of our society is changing in certain ways which we do not properly understand; there is a distinct possibility that even if we understand them we should not be able to respond to them.

Political systems do not exist in a vacuum. They exist in the context of, and are sustained by, social institutions, and it is not possible for a society to maintain just any structure of politics or to ensure to its citizens a system of rights and freedoms simply by wishing it were so. Such benefits are necessarily rooted in specific contexts. As Edmund Burke observed, the rights of an Englishman are better founded than the Rights of Man. It is therefore entirely possible that the structure of economic powers in our society and the increasing interdependence of our political, economic, educational and social institutions should lead us to a position where our rhetoric of pluralistic democracy shall cease to bear any but the most tangential relation to reality.

CONCLUSION

It is entirely understandable that it should be radical students of the social sciences who should respond earliest and most alarmingly to these hinted developments. Radicals are more likely to react to likely developments of an economic determinism than are conservatives; students are more likely to translate their premonitions into action than sections of the population who have less freedom. And students of the social sciences are more likely than others to be aware of potential developments in social and political affairs.

Disillusion with governing parties of the left is as predictable among radical students as the succession of night by day.

However, it is still a matter of interest to know the precise form this disillusion takes, and the precise alternatives that are proffered by it. In the present case the disillusion is with the whole edifice of rational calculation and systematisation that has sustained the development of western culture and the emergence of industrialism. And the alternative that seems to be offered is, logically, a rejection of these forms of activity and a reaction against the apparently discredited structure of pluralistic politics. We are called upon to embrace a new totality, a new mass revolution designed to erect a society of creative spontaneity in which there is social harmony without social control, social co-ordination without government, co-operation without conflict. In short, it is the re-emergence of the messianic dream.[25]

Although this characterisation involves a negative view of the political contribution of the revolt, seeing it as essentially existing outside the realm of political reality, we should acknowledge its positive aspects. The student movement has drawn attention to various emerging problems for the politics of the advanced western world, and no one who is concerned for the future stability of our pluralism, democracy and civil liberty can but be deeply interested in these matters. It is unfortunate that the doings of the student revolutionaries have attracted far more public curiosity and anxiety than the problems to which they can be seen as an understandable though unfruitful reaction.

My reasons for considering their response unfruitful should by now be clear. They can most succinctly be summarised by concluding that the main import of the student revolutionaries' distinctive proposals for the improvement of our world are this: that we should organise our society in all its aspects according to principles that are by nature transitory and incapable of institutionalisation. This gives, I suggest, full credit to the revolutionary nature of the proposal, and a fair indication of its likely chances of success.

REFERENCES

1. Schmalenbach, H., *The Sociological Category of Communion*, 1922 (trans. Naegele, K. D., and Stone, G. P.)
2. Duverger, M., *Political Parties*, p 124 *et seq*
3. *viz* such works as Robinson, J. A. T., *Honest to God*, 1963, and the various writings which influenced them
4. Roszak, T., *The Making of a Counter-Culture*, 1970, esp. Ch IV
5. Hall, S., "The Hippies: An American 'Moment'" (in Nagel, J. (ed), *Student Power*, 1969)
6. Lowenthal, R., "Unreason and Revolution" (*Encounter*, November, 1969)
7. Mannheim, K., *Ideology and Utopia*, 1936
8. Weber, M., *Science as a Vocation*, 1918
9. Galbraith, J. K., *The New Industrial State*, 1967
10. Westergaard, J., "The Withering Away of Class" (in Anderson, P. and Blackburn, R., *Towards Socialism*, 1965)
11. Abrams, M., *Must Labour Lose?*, 1960
12. Crosland, A., *The Future of Socialism*, 1956
13. Galbraith, J. K., *The Affluent Society*, 1958
14. Crosland, *op cit*
15. Wilson, H., Speech at Labour Party Conference, Scarborough, 1963
16. An interesting study of this process in a single area of policy is Eckstein, H., *The English Health Service*, 1958
17. Wilson, H., Speech at Swansea, January 25, 1964
18. The National Plan, 1965
19. Abel-Smith, B., *Labour's Social Plans*, Fabian Society, 1967
20. Crosland, *op cit*
21. Abel-Smith, *op cit*
22. Radice, G. and Edmunds, J., *Low Pay*, Fabian Society, 1968
23. MacIntyre, A., "The Strange Death of Social Democratic England" (*The Listener*, July 4 1968)
24. Wilson, H., Scarborough Speech, *op cit*
25. For an excellent discussion of these themes from a position largely sympathetic to the revolt, see Roszak, *op cit*

Index

Index

245